# Excel Basic Skills

Year 4

Ages 9–10

# English and Mathematics

PASCAL PRESS

# Contents

# Introduction

The ***Excel*** **Basic Skills Workbook** series aims to build and reinforce basic skills in reading, comprehension and mathematics.

The series has eight English and Mathematics core books, one for each of the school years Kindergarten/Foundation to Year 7. These are supported by teaching books, which can be used if the student needs help in a particular area of study.

## The structure of this book

**This book has 30 carefully sequenced double-page units.** Each unit has work on Number and Algebra, Measurement and Geometry, and Statistics and Probability in Maths, and Reading and Comprehension, Spelling and Vocabulary, and Grammar and Punctuation in English.

The student's competence in each of the 30 units can be recorded on the marking grid on pages 5 and 7. There are four end-of-term reviews. These are referred to as Tests 1 to 4. They assess the student's understanding of work covered during each term.

## How to use this book

It is recommended that students complete each unit in the sequence provided because the knowledge and understanding developed in each unit is consolidated and practised in subsequent units. The workbook can be used to cover core classroom work. It can also be used to provide homework and consolidation activities.

All units are written so that particular questions deal with the same areas of learning in each unit. For example, question 1 is always on Number (addition) and question 11 is always on Measurement (time), and so on. Similarly in the English units question 1 is always on Reading and Comprehension, and question 14 is always on Punctuation. Question formatting is repeated throughout the workbook to support familiarity so that students can more readily deal with the Mathematics and English content.

The marking grids (see the examples on pages 4 and 6) are easy-to-use tools for recording students' progress. If you find that certain questions are repeatedly causing difficulties and errors, then there is a specific ***Excel*** **Basic/Advanced Skills Workbook** to help students fully revise that topic.

These are the teaching books of the series; they will take students through the topic step by step. The use of illustrations and diagrams, practice questions, and a straightforward and simple approach will make some of the most common problem areas of English and Mathematics easy to understand and master.

# Sample Maths Marking Grid

If a student is consistently getting more than **one in five** questions wrong in any area, refer to the highlighted ***Excel*** **Basic/Advanced Skills** title. When marking answers on the grid, simply mark incorrect answers with 'X' in the appropriate box. This will result in a graphical representation of areas needing further work. An example has been done below for the first seven units. If a question has several parts, it should be counted as wrong if one or more mistakes are made.

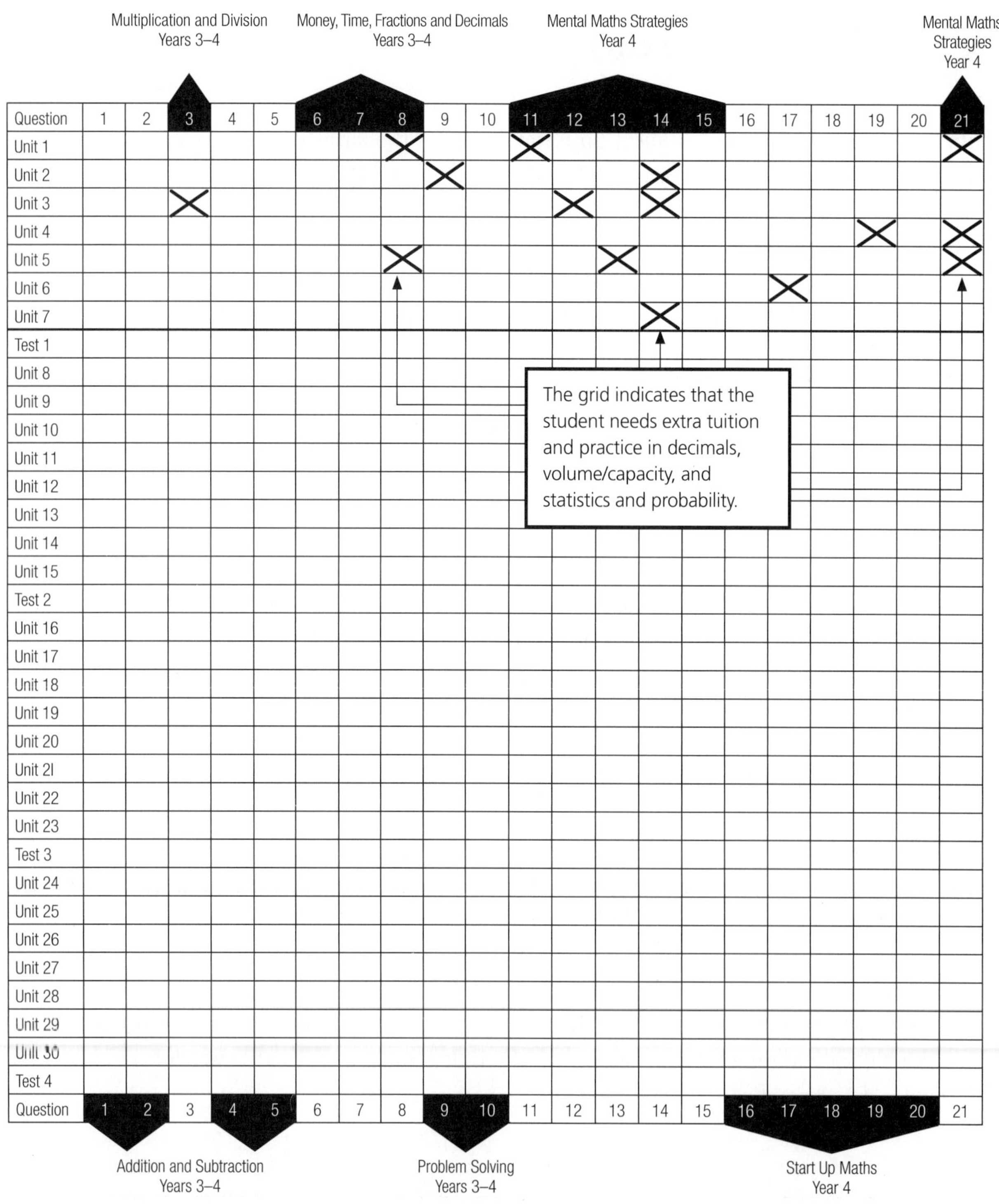


| Question | 1 | 2 | 3 | 4 | 5 | 6 | 7 | 8 | 9 | 10 | 11 | 12 | 13 | 14 | 15 | 16 | 17 | 18 | 19 | 20 | 21 |
|---|---|---|---|---|---|---|---|---|---|---|---|---|---|---|---|---|---|---|---|---|---|
| Unit 1 | | | | | | | | X | | | X | | | | | | | | | | X |
| Unit 2 | | | | | | | | | X | | | | | X | | | | | | | |
| Unit 3 | | | X | | | | | | | | | X | | X | | | | | | | |
| Unit 4 | | | | | | | | | | | | | | | | | | | X | | X |
| Unit 5 | | | | | | | | X | | | | | X | | | | | | | | X |
| Unit 6 | | | | | | | | | | | | | | | | | X | | | | |
| Unit 7 | | | | | | | | | | | | | | X | | | | | | | |
| Test 1 | | | | | | | | | | | | | | | | | | | | | |
| Unit 8 | | | | | | | | | | | | | | | | | | | | | |
| Unit 9 | | | | | | | | | | | | | | | | | | | | | |
| Unit 10 | | | | | | | | | | | | | | | | | | | | | |
| Unit 11 | | | | | | | | | | | | | | | | | | | | | |
| Unit 12 | | | | | | | | | | | | | | | | | | | | | |
| Unit 13 | | | | | | | | | | | | | | | | | | | | | |
| Unit 14 | | | | | | | | | | | | | | | | | | | | | |
| Unit 15 | | | | | | | | | | | | | | | | | | | | | |
| Test 2 | | | | | | | | | | | | | | | | | | | | | |
| Unit 16 | | | | | | | | | | | | | | | | | | | | | |
| Unit 17 | | | | | | | | | | | | | | | | | | | | | |
| Unit 18 | | | | | | | | | | | | | | | | | | | | | |
| Unit 19 | | | | | | | | | | | | | | | | | | | | | |
| Unit 20 | | | | | | | | | | | | | | | | | | | | | |
| Unit 21 | | | | | | | | | | | | | | | | | | | | | |
| Unit 22 | | | | | | | | | | | | | | | | | | | | | |
| Unit 23 | | | | | | | | | | | | | | | | | | | | | |
| Test 3 | | | | | | | | | | | | | | | | | | | | | |
| Unit 24 | | | | | | | | | | | | | | | | | | | | | |
| Unit 25 | | | | | | | | | | | | | | | | | | | | | |
| Unit 26 | | | | | | | | | | | | | | | | | | | | | |
| Unit 27 | | | | | | | | | | | | | | | | | | | | | |
| Unit 28 | | | | | | | | | | | | | | | | | | | | | |
| Unit 29 | | | | | | | | | | | | | | | | | | | | | |
| Unit 30 | | | | | | | | | | | | | | | | | | | | | |
| Test 4 | | | | | | | | | | | | | | | | | | | | | |
| Question | 1 | 2 | 3 | 4 | 5 | 6 | 7 | 8 | 9 | 10 | 11 | 12 | 13 | 14 | 15 | 16 | 17 | 18 | 19 | 20 | 21 |

# Maths Marking Grid

| | Addition | Subtraction | Division/ Multiplication | Place Value | Number Patterns | Fractions | Money | Decimals | Estimating | Problem Solving | Time | Mass/ Length | Area | Volume/ Capacity | Temperature | 2D Shapes | 3D Shapes | Angles | Symmetry/ Transformation | Direction | Statistics and Probability |
|---|---|---|---|---|---|---|---|---|---|---|---|---|---|---|---|---|---|---|---|---|---|
| Question | 1 | 2 | 3 | 4 | 5 | 6 | 7 | 8 | 9 | 10 | 11 | 12 | 13 | 14 | 15 | 16 | 17 | 18 | 19 | 20 | 21 |
| Unit 1 | | | | | | | | | | | | | | | | | | | | | |
| Unit 2 | | | | | | | | | | | | | | | | | | | | | |
| Unit 3 | | | | | | | | | | | | | | | | | | | | | |
| Unit 4 | | | | | | | | | | | | | | | | | | | | | |
| Unit 5 | | | | | | | | | | | | | | | | | | | | | |
| Unit 6 | | | | | | | | | | | | | | | | | | | | | |
| Unit 7 | | | | | | | | | | | | | | | | | | | | | |
| Test 1 | | | | | | | | | | | | | | | | | | | | | |
| Unit 8 | | | | | | | | | | | | | | | | | | | | | |
| Unit 9 | | | | | | | | | | | | | | | | | | | | | |
| Unit 10 | | | | | | | | | | | | | | | | | | | | | |
| Unit 11 | | | | | | | | | | | | | | | | | | | | | |
| Unit 12 | | | | | | | | | | | | | | | | | | | | | |
| Unit 13 | | | | | | | | | | | | | | | | | | | | | |
| Unit 14 | | | | | | | | | | | | | | | | | | | | | |
| Unit 15 | | | | | | | | | | | | | | | | | | | | | |
| Test 2 | | | | | | | | | | | | | | | | | | | | | |
| Unit 16 | | | | | | | | | | | | | | | | | | | | | |
| Unit 17 | | | | | | | | | | | | | | | | | | | | | |
| Unit 18 | | | | | | | | | | | | | | | | | | | | | |
| Unit 19 | | | | | | | | | | | | | | | | | | | | | |
| Unit 20 | | | | | | | | | | | | | | | | | | | | | |
| Unit 21 | | | | | | | | | | | | | | | | | | | | | |
| Unit 22 | | | | | | | | | | | | | | | | | | | | | |
| Unit 23 | | | | | | | | | | | | | | | | | | | | | |
| Test 3 | | | | | | | | | | | | | | | | | | | | | |
| Unit 24 | | | | | | | | | | | | | | | | | | | | | |
| Unit 25 | | | | | | | | | | | | | | | | | | | | | |
| Unit 26 | | | | | | | | | | | | | | | | | | | | | |
| Unit 27 | | | | | | | | | | | | | | | | | | | | | |
| Unit 28 | | | | | | | | | | | | | | | | | | | | | |
| Unit 29 | | | | | | | | | | | | | | | | | | | | | |
| Unit 30 | | | | | | | | | | | | | | | | | | | | | |
| Test 4 | | | | | | | | | | | | | | | | | | | | | |
| Question | 1 | 2 | 3 | 4 | 5 | 6 | 7 | 8 | 9 | 10 | 11 | 12 | 13 | 14 | 15 | 16 | 17 | 18 | 19 | 20 | 21 |

# Sample English Marking Grid

If a student is consistently getting more than **one in five** questions wrong in any area, refer to the highlighted ***Excel*** **Advanced Skills** title. When marking answers on the grid, simply mark incorrect answers with 'X' in the appropriate box. This will result in a graphical representation of areas needing further work. An example has been done below for the first seven units.

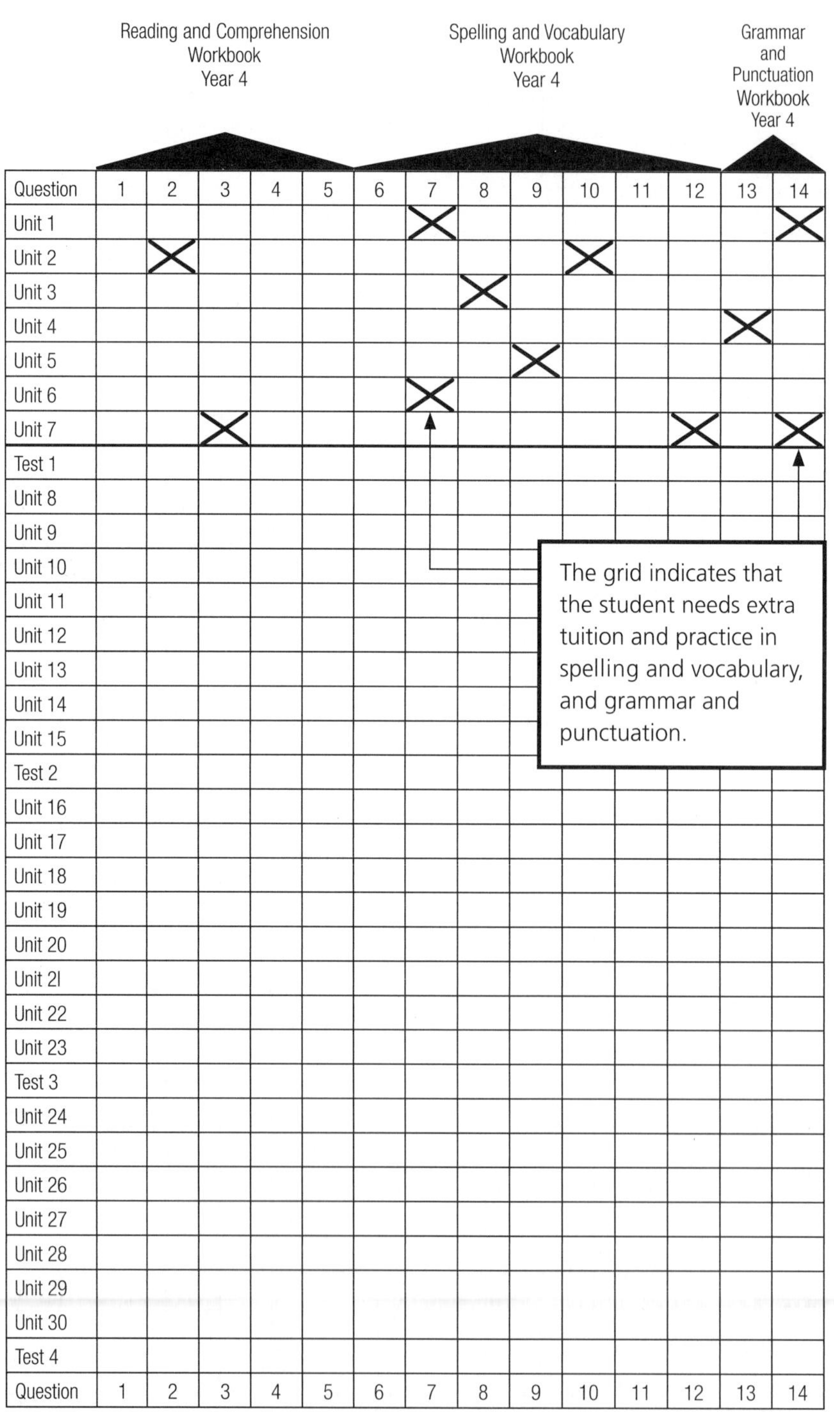

| | Reading and Comprehension Workbook Year 4 | | | | | Spelling and Vocabulary Workbook Year 4 | | | | | | | Grammar and Punctuation Workbook Year 4 | |
|---|---|---|---|---|---|---|---|---|---|---|---|---|---|---|
| Question | 1 | 2 | 3 | 4 | 5 | 6 | 7 | 8 | 9 | 10 | 11 | 12 | 13 | 14 |
| Unit 1 | | | | | | | X | | | | | | | X |
| Unit 2 | | X | | | | | | | | X | | | | |
| Unit 3 | | | | | | | | X | | | | | | |
| Unit 4 | | | | | | | | | | | | | X | |
| Unit 5 | | | | | | | | | X | | | | | |
| Unit 6 | | | | | | | X | | | | | | | |
| Unit 7 | | | X | | | | | | | | | X | | X |
| Test 1 | | | | | | | | | | | | | | |
| Unit 8 | | | | | | | | | | | | | | |
| Unit 9 | | | | | | | | | | | | | | |
| Unit 10 | | | | | | | | | | | | | | |
| Unit 11 | | | | | | | | | | | | | | |
| Unit 12 | | | | | | | | | | | | | | |
| Unit 13 | | | | | | | | | | | | | | |
| Unit 14 | | | | | | | | | | | | | | |
| Unit 15 | | | | | | | | | | | | | | |
| Test 2 | | | | | | | | | | | | | | |
| Unit 16 | | | | | | | | | | | | | | |
| Unit 17 | | | | | | | | | | | | | | |
| Unit 18 | | | | | | | | | | | | | | |
| Unit 19 | | | | | | | | | | | | | | |
| Unit 20 | | | | | | | | | | | | | | |
| Unit 21 | | | | | | | | | | | | | | |
| Unit 22 | | | | | | | | | | | | | | |
| Unit 23 | | | | | | | | | | | | | | |
| Test 3 | | | | | | | | | | | | | | |
| Unit 24 | | | | | | | | | | | | | | |
| Unit 25 | | | | | | | | | | | | | | |
| Unit 26 | | | | | | | | | | | | | | |
| Unit 27 | | | | | | | | | | | | | | |
| Unit 28 | | | | | | | | | | | | | | |
| Unit 29 | | | | | | | | | | | | | | |
| Unit 30 | | | | | | | | | | | | | | |
| Test 4 | | | | | | | | | | | | | | |
| Question | 1 | 2 | 3 | 4 | 5 | 6 | 7 | 8 | 9 | 10 | 11 | 12 | 13 | 14 |

The grid indicates that the student needs extra tuition and practice in spelling and vocabulary, and grammar and punctuation.

# English Marking Grid

| | Reading and Comprehension | | | | | Spelling and Vocabulary | | | | | | | Grammar and Punctuation | |
|---|---|---|---|---|---|---|---|---|---|---|---|---|---|---|
| Question | 1 | 2 | 3 | 4 | 5 | 6 | 7 | 8 | 9 | 10 | 11 | 12 | 13 | 14 |
| Unit 1 | | | | | | | | | | | | | | |
| Unit 2 | | | | | | | | | | | | | | |
| Unit 3 | | | | | | | | | | | | | | |
| Unit 4 | | | | | | | | | | | | | | |
| Unit 5 | | | | | | | | | | | | | | |
| Unit 6 | | | | | | | | | | | | | | |
| Unit 7 | | | | | | | | | | | | | | |
| Test 1 | | | | | | | | | | | | | | |
| Unit 8 | | | | | | | | | | | | | | |
| Unit 9 | | | | | | | | | | | | | | |
| Unit 10 | | | | | | | | | | | | | | |
| Unit 11 | | | | | | | | | | | | | | |
| Unit 12 | | | | | | | | | | | | | | |
| Unit 13 | | | | | | | | | | | | | | |
| Unit 14 | | | | | | | | | | | | | | |
| Unit 15 | | | | | | | | | | | | | | |
| Test 2 | | | | | | | | | | | | | | |
| Unit 16 | | | | | | | | | | | | | | |
| Unit 17 | | | | | | | | | | | | | | |
| Unit 18 | | | | | | | | | | | | | | |
| Unit 19 | | | | | | | | | | | | | | |
| Unit 20 | | | | | | | | | | | | | | |
| Unit 21 | | | | | | | | | | | | | | |
| Unit 22 | | | | | | | | | | | | | | |
| Unit 23 | | | | | | | | | | | | | | |
| Test 3 | | | | | | | | | | | | | | |
| Unit 24 | | | | | | | | | | | | | | |
| Unit 25 | | | | | | | | | | | | | | |
| Unit 26 | | | | | | | | | | | | | | |
| Unit 27 | | | | | | | | | | | | | | |
| Unit 28 | | | | | | | | | | | | | | |
| Unit 29 | | | | | | | | | | | | | | |
| Unit 30 | | | | | | | | | | | | | | |
| Test 4 | | | | | | | | | | | | | | |
| Question | 1 | 2 | 3 | 4 | 5 | 6 | 7 | 8 | 9 | 10 | 11 | 12 | 13 | 14 |

## Number and Algebra

1.

| + | 3 | 8 | 0 | 12 | 6 | 18 |
|---|---|---|---|---|---|---|
| 3 | | | | | | |

2.

| – | 4 | 15 | 18 | 9 | 10 | 23 |
|---|---|---|---|---|---|---|
| 3 | | | | | | |

3.

| × | 8 | 7 | 6 | 5 | 4 | 10 |
|---|---|---|---|---|---|---|
| 3 | | | | | | |

4. Write the number for sixty-eight ones.

5. Complete the pattern of odd numbers.

13, 15, 17, ☐, ☐, ☐, ☐, ☐

6. Colour part of each group to match the fraction given.

(a) 2 out of 3 (b) 4 sixths

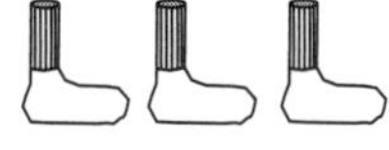

7. Write these in decimal form.

(a) 30c ☐ (b) 5c ☐

8. Write the decimal shown by this model.

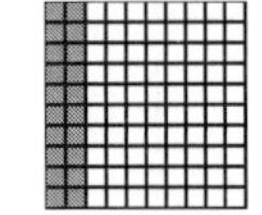

9. Is 187 closer to 100 or 200?

10. Six girls had five yo-yos each. How many yo-yos are there altogether?

## Measurement and Geometry

11. Complete the labels for the time shown.

11:

past

12. Use the short form to write:

(a) 12 kilograms

(b) twenty kilograms

13. Circle the things with a surface area more than a square metre.
blackboard, kitchen floor, book cover, envelope

14. How many 1 L milk cartons could fill this bucket?

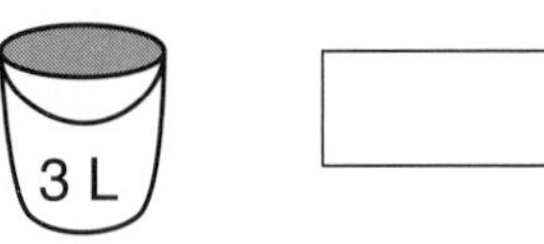


15. Make this thermometer to the 'hot' level.

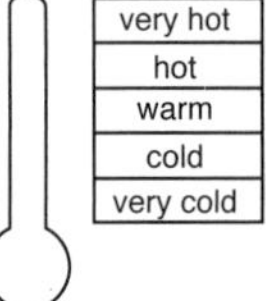


16. Name this shape.

17. How many corners does this shape have?

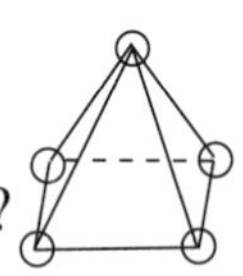

18. Are these angles the same size?

A B

19. Draw in the axes of symmetry.

20. Whose place is the third from the left?

| Ben | Rajiv | Mick | Anna | Tom | Lisa |
|---|---|---|---|---|---|

## Statistics and Probability

21. How many seals did Sophia see at the zoo?

| Seal | 卌 卌 | Elephant | 卌 III |
|---|---|---|---|
| Koala | III | Lion | II |

## Mr MacDonald's Fruit Market

Best Quality—Best Prices
Under New Management

A Real Bargain
Navel Oranges
3 kg Net Bags
$1.59
EVERY DAY

Tomatoes Firm
Top Grade
55c/kg
EVERY DAY

Large Lettuce
39c each
$4.50 / box

Extra Large Celery
79c per bunch
$8 per box

A REAL BARGAIN
Golden Sweet
Corn
4 for 99c
Friday only

A Real Bargain
Red Delicious
Apples Large Size
59c per kg
THURSDAY ONLY

Extra Large Eggs
$1.89
dozen

Fresh Broccoli
79c/kg

## Reading and Comprehension

**1.** How many eggs would I get for $1.89?
(a) 8 (b) 6
(c) 12 (d) 9

**2.** On which day can I buy the corn at the cheap price of ninety-nine cents?
(a) every day (b) Thursday
(c) weekends only (d) Friday

**3.** At seventy-nine cents a kilogram, I would be purchasing
(a) apples. (b) lettuce.
(c) celery. (d) broccoli.

**4.** How much would two kilograms of tomatoes cost?

____________________________________

**5.** Number these fruits and vegetables in alphabetical order (1–6).
(a) apples (b) tomatoes
(c) celery (d) corn
(e) broccoli (f) lettuce

## Spelling and Vocabulary

Rewrite the misspelt words.

**6.** Our Art teacha showed us how to make candles. ________________

**7.** Read the label on the medacin bottle carefully.

____________________________________

Circle the word that has the nearest meaning to the underlined word.

**8.** The sign read: Beware of <u>fierce</u> dog!
(a) foul (b) savage
(c) sick (d) funny

**9.** After football training, I was so <u>tired</u> that I went straight to bed.
(a) tense (b) thrilled
(c) exhausted (d) fit

Circle the correct word in brackets.

**10.** It rained (real, really) heavily this morning.

**11.** (Who's, Whose) pencil case is this?

**12.** She works (neatly, neat) on every task she is given.

## Grammar and Punctuation

**13.** Underline the **nouns** in these sentences.

The largest dinosaur was the Brachiosaurus. It was nearly twenty-four metres long and its head could stretch seventeen metres above the ground.

**14.** Punctuate and capitalise this sentence.

rectangles and trapeziums are both quadrilaterals

____________________________________

____________________________________

## Number and Algebra

1.

| + | 10 | 15 | 1 | 9 | 13 | 19 |
|---|---|---|---|---|---|---|
| 1 | | | | | | |

2.

| − | 1 | 10 | 7 | 18 | 11 | 20 |
|---|---|---|---|---|---|---|
| 1 | | | | | | |

3.

| ÷ | 1 | 5 | 10 | 7 | 20 | 21 |
|---|---|---|---|---|---|---|
| 1 | | | | | | |

4. Write the number for 3 tens and 9 ones.

5. Complete the pattern of even numbers.

44, 48, ___, ___, ___, ___, ___

6. What part is coloured?

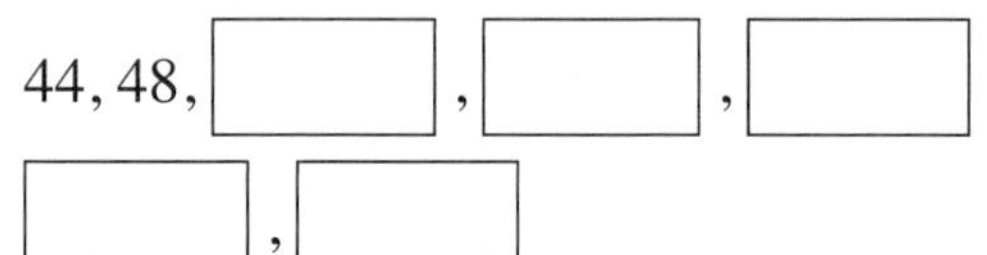

___ eights

7. Write these amounts in decimal form.

(a) 55c ___ (b) 10c ___

(c) 95c ___

8. Write the decimal shown by this model.

9. Is 612 closer to 600 or 700?

10. A farmer had 97 cows but sold 25. How many cows did he have left?

## Measurement and Geometry

11. Write the time that is 1 minute after:

(a) 3:19 ___ (b) 9:04 ___

12. Circle the words for objects that have a mass greater than 1 kilogram.
nail, brick, tennis ball, marble, dog

13. True or False?
The area of the top of my lunchbox is more than a square metre.

14. What is the total capacity of this set of containers?

15. We use a

__ h __ __ __ om __ __ __ __

to measure temperature.

16. Circle the quadrilateral.

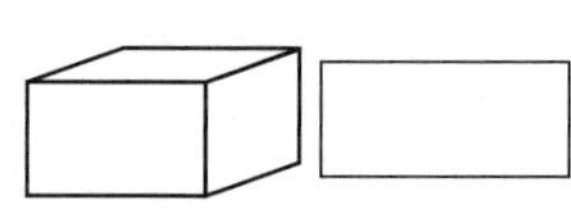

17. How many corners does this rectangular prism have?

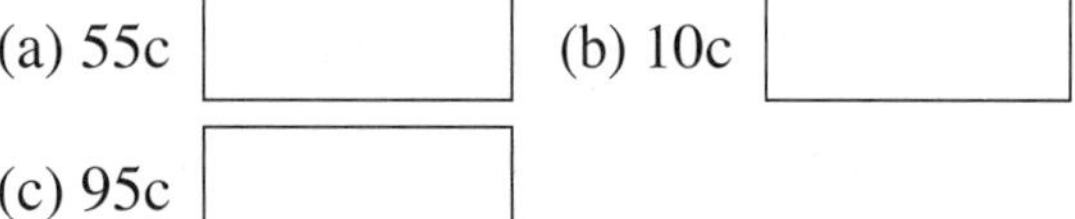

18. Which angle is the smallest?

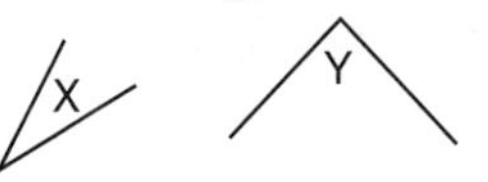


19. How many axes of symmetry does this shape have?

20. Which shelf is the skateboard on?

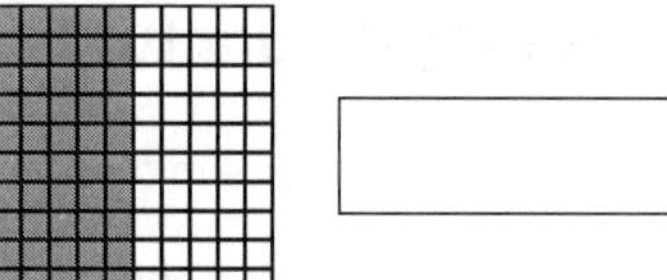

## Statistics and Probability

21. How many ice-creams did Lucas eat in January?

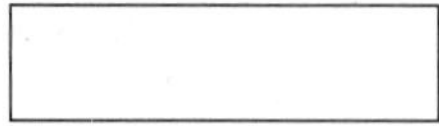

**SINEPOST STATE SCHOOL FETE**
Saturday, 10 October 2013
3:00 pm to 9:00 pm

**Entertainment Programme**

| | | |
|---|---|---|
| 3:00 | pm | Devonshire Tea (Music Room) |
| 3:30 | pm | Year 2 Bushdancing |
| 4:00 | pm | School Band (Assembly Hall) |
| 4:30 | pm | Preschool Play |
| 5:00 | pm | Year 6/7 Disco begins |
| 5:30 | pm | BBQ (Tuckshop area) |
| 6:00 | pm | Ethnic Dancing display |
| 6:30 | pm | Book Competition Winners |
| 7:00 | pm | Fireworks Display |
| 7:30 | pm | Fancy Dress Ball |

Come along and enjoy the day ...
Multicultural Food Stalls ...

## Reading and Comprehension

1. At what time does the Bushdance begin?
(a) 7 pm (b) 5:30 pm
(c) 3:30 pm (d) 6:00 pm

2. Which food item would you expect to eat at a Devonshire Tea?
(a) chicken soup (b) devon
(c) scones with jam (d) souvlakia

3. Which of these would be a suitable time to arrive at the Fete?
(a) 11 o'clock (b) 8:00 pm
(c) 3:30 pm (d) 7:30 pm

4. Whereabouts in the schoolground is the barbecue going to take place?

________________________________

5. Number these events in the correct programme order (1–5).
(a) Fireworks Display
(b) Ethnic Dancing
(c) Fancy Dress Ball
(d) School Band
(e) Preschool Play

## Spelling and Vocabulary

Rewrite the misspelt words.

6. We found a massage in a bottle.

________________________________

7. He spred too much butter on my roll.

________________________________

Circle the word that has the nearest meaning to the underlined word.

8. "Let that be a <u>lesson</u> to you," stated Mr Bobbymore.
(a) thought
(b) trick
(c) learning
(d) example

9. My job on Saturday is to <u>receive</u> the guests.
(a) greet
(b) give
(c) take
(d) match

Circle the correct word in brackets.

10. This box is particularly (heavy, heavier).

11. I (missed, mist) your birthday by two days.

12. It's taken two weeks for my injury to (heal, heel).

## Grammar and Punctuation

13. Underline the **verbs** in these sentences.

A track led off through the bush so I decided to follow it. At last I came to Ned's farm.

14. Punctuate and capitalise this sentence.

how many times do i have to tell you to tidy your room bellowed mum

________________________________

________________________________

________________________________

## Number and Algebra

1.

| + | 12 | 8 | 7 | 3 | 0 | 50 |
|---|---|---|---|---|---|---|
| 0 | | | | | | |

2.

| – | 5 | 12 | 6 | 8 | 11 | 50 |
|---|---|---|---|---|---|---|
| 0 | | | | | | |

3.

| × | 0 | 8 | 3 | 2 | 1 | 50 |
|---|---|---|---|---|---|---|
| 0 | | | | | | |

4. Write the number for one hundred and sixty-four.

5. Complete the pattern of even numbers.

88, 90, ___, ___, ___, ___, ___

6. What part of the group is coloured?

___ fifth

7. Write the amounts as cents.

(a) $0.60 ___ (b) $0.40 ___

8. Complete these labels.

(a) 70 hundredths ___

(b) 30 hundredths ___

(c) 90 hundredths ___

9. Round off 456 to the nearest hundred.

10. Errol had 49 basketball cards and bought 12 more. How many cards altogether?

## Measurement and Geometry

11. Write the time that is five minutes after:

(a) 10:53 ___ (b) 5:55 ___

12. What's the total mass of cheese and meat?

13. What is the area of this shape?

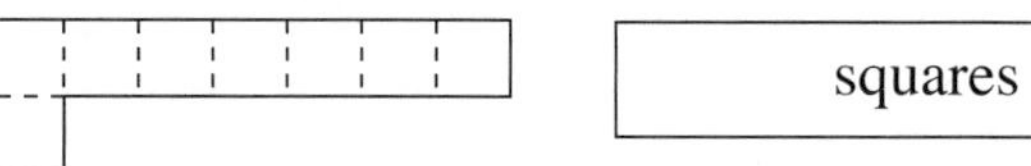

___ squares

14. If there are 4 cups of milk in one litre, then how many would be in three litres?

15. Use the short form to write fifty degrees Celsius.

16. Circle the triangle which has 2 sides equal?

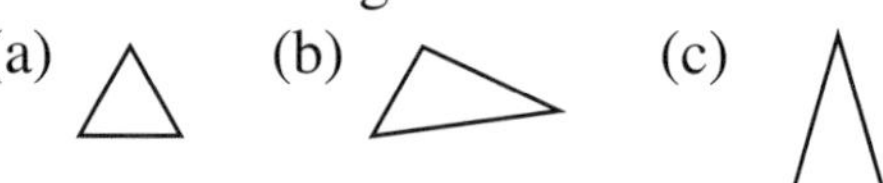


17. How many faces in this object?

18. Draw a right angle.

19. How many axes of symmetry does this shape have?

20. Name the fruit in the box that is middle, top.

## Statistics and Probability

21. How many apples were bought in March?

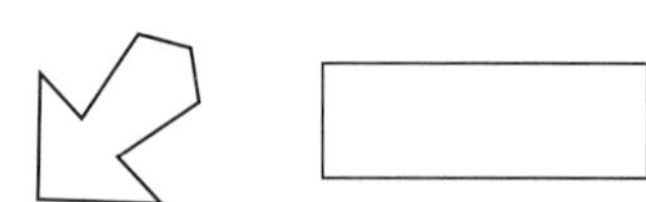

## Reading and Comprehension

1. Mrs Jones lives in Broken Hill. In which state does she live?
   (a) Queensland (b) New South Wales
   (c) Victoria (d) Tasmania

2. In which direction is Sydney from Perth?
   (a) North (b) East
   (c) South (d) West

3. What is the capital city of Queensland?
   (a) Cairns (b) Rockhampton
   (c) Mount Isa (d) Brisbane

4. What do the letters NT stand for?

   ______________________________

5. Number these state names in alphabetical order (1–6).
   (a) Queensland (b) Tasmania
   (c) Victoria (d) South Australia
   (e) Western Australia (f) New South Wales

## Spelling and Vocabulary

Rewrite the misspelt words.

6. Linda has wondafull memories of her birthday party.

   ______________________________

7. Eating lots of fruit is good for your healf.

   ______________________________

Circle the word that has the nearest meaning to the underlined word.

8. <u>Wheel</u> the barrow this way, please Annie!
   (a) wander (b) push
   (c) welcome (d) wave

9. Ladies and gentlemen, I <u>present</u> to you the School Captain.
   (a) welcome (b) introduce
   (c) throne (d) speak

Circle the correct word in brackets.

10. The (heir, air) around us is getting more and more polluted.

11. Most cities are choked with (trathic, traffic) jams

12. Every snowflake has a (difference, different) pattern.

## Grammar and Punctuation

13. Underline the **adjectives** in these sentences.

    My shoes were covered in thick mud. My tired legs were scratched and bitten. I hopped to the sick room immediately.

14. Punctuate and capitalise this sentence.

    im not sure about david simon kevin or michael

    ______________________________

    ______________________________

## Number and Algebra

1.

| + | 3 | 7 | 8 | 10 | 4 | 12 |
|---|---|---|---|---|---|---|
| 8 | | | | | | |

2.

| – | 8 | 20 | 11 | 15 | 13 | 26 |
|---|---|---|---|---|---|---|
| 8 | | | | | | |

3.

| ÷ | 16 | 32 | 80 | 48 | 24 | 88 |
|---|---|---|---|---|---|---|
| 8 | | | | | | |

**4.** Write the number for seven hundred and nine. [ ]

**5.** Complete the pattern of odd numbers.

59, [ ], [ ], 65, [ ], [ ], [ ]

**6.** Complete the label below.

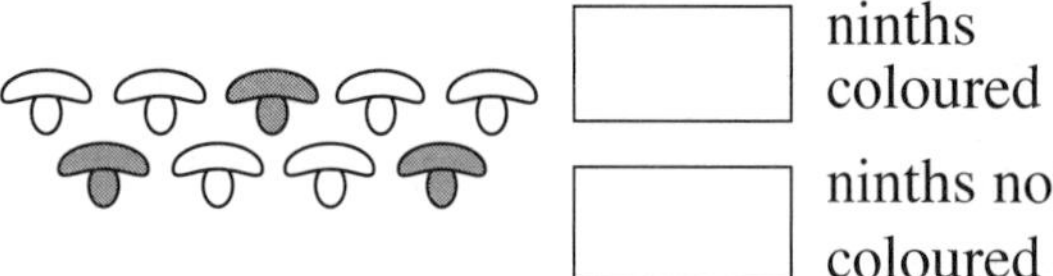

[ ] ninths coloured

[ ] ninths not coloured

**7.** Find the total for each.

(a) 10c + 5c [ ]

(b) $0.50 + $0.20 [ ]

**8.** In this hundred square, colour the fraction shown.
70 hundredths

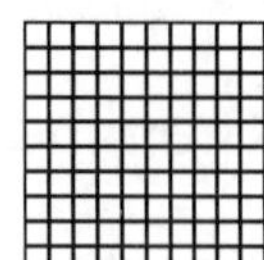

**9.** Round off 379 to the nearest hundred. [ ]

**10.** Billy has to use three stones to cross the creek from left to right. Find the number of paths he could take.

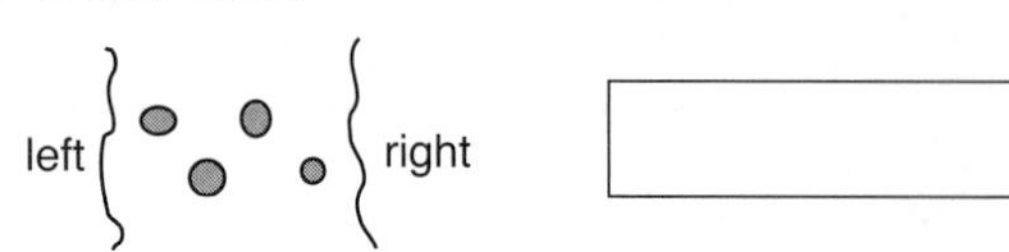


[ ]

## Measurement and Geometry

**11.** Complete the labels for these times.

(a) **6 : 09** ____ past ____

(b) **10 : 38** ____ past ____

**12.** Which of these are correctly written? Circle them.
19 kg, 14 KG, 49 kg, 49 kgs, 10 kG

**13.** Circle the best answer.
How many children could stand in a one-square-metre space?
only 4, 16, 52, probably 7, 100

**14.** Circle the objects that would hold less than a litre.
bath tub, eggcup, teaspoon, glass, pool

**15.** Circle the highest temperature.
75°C, 65°C, 45°C, 91°C, 25°C

**16.** How many sides does this shape have? [ ]

**17.** How many corners does a cube have? [ ]

**18.** The size of an angle is the amount of
_ _ _ _ _ _ _ between its arms.

**19.** One <u>axis</u> of symmetry … two _ _ _ _ of symmetry.

**20.** Write the position of the grapes. [ ]

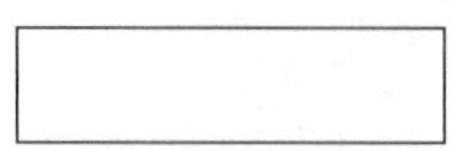

## Statistics and Probability

**21.** How many figures are wearing shoes? [ ]

# Sundale Teacher Shines

Sundale State School teacher Mary Simons has been named Teacher of the Year in the 2012 Apple Professional Australian Teacher Awards. The winner was announced last Friday night in Brisbane and twenty-nine-year-old Mary beat a team of 300 nominees to the title.

Mary has worked as a teacher in Queensland since 2003 and had been judged on dedication, work attitude, approach to work and lesson creativity.

"I was a bit surprised when one of my Year 4 students told me that she had filled in the form and sent it in. At first, I thought she was joking," said the modest prize winner.

Her prize includes a two-week holiday in Auckland (NZ) and the chance to study overseas at Harvard University in the USA. She also received a large carton of chocolate frogs which she promises to share with her twenty-six students.

## Reading and Comprehension

1. In which Australian state was the awards ceremony held?
   (a) Auckland
   (b) Brisbane
   (c) USA
   (d) Queensland

2. *Modest* means
   (a) 'arrogant'. (b) 'bold'.
   (c) 'forward'. (d) 'bashful'.

3. How old is Ms Simons?
   (a) 26 (b) 29
   (c) 30 (d) It doesn't mention her age.

4. On which four aspects of her teaching was she judged?

   ______________________________

   ______________________________

5. Number these sentences in order (1–4).
   (a) Her prize consisted of a holiday.
   (b) Mary works at Sundale Primary.
   (c) She beat 300 other teachers.
   (d) She has worked in Queensland since 2003.

## Spelling and Vocabulary

Rewrite the misspelt words.

6. The Tanami Dessert is in Australia.

   ______________________________

7. My famlee consists of Mum, my brother and me. ______________

Circle the word that has the nearest meaning to the underlined word.

8. The King's <u>throne</u> was made out of solid gold.
   (a) spoon (b) crown
   (c) chair (d) drum

9. The baby hasn't <u>touched</u> his mashed potato.
   (a) taken (b) mastered
   (c) burped (d) wanted

Circle the correct word in the brackets.

10. Two explorers raced to (reaching, reach) the South Pole first.

11. The world's biggest (flower, flour) may not be the prettiest one!

12. The Statue of Liberty (stood, stands) on an island in New York Harbour.

## Grammar and Punctuation

13. Underline the **pronouns** in these sentences.

    I shook my head. There were at least five children around me, not listening. Someone was going to find themselves in big trouble—soon!

14. Punctuate and capitalise this sentence.

    where did you put my soccer jersey asked the boy politely

    ______________________________

    ______________________________

## Number and Algebra

1.

| + | 1 | 5 | 4 | 3 | 8 | 11 |
|---|---|---|---|---|---|---|
| 9 | | | | | | |

2.

| – | 9 | 15 | 16 | 19 | 10 | 18 |
|---|---|---|---|---|---|---|
| 9 | | | | | | |

3.

| × | 3 | 9 | 6 | 2 | 7 | 10 |
|---|---|---|---|---|---|---|
| 9 | | | | | | |

4. What is the number shown on this abacus?

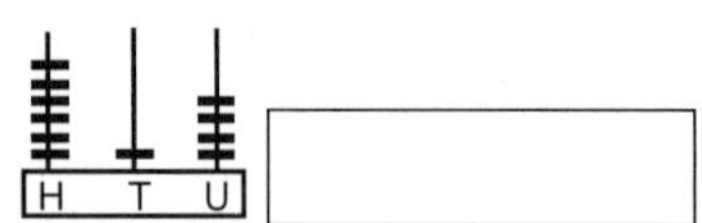

5. Write in the missing numbers.
981, 982, 983, ___, ___, ___, ___, ___

6. Complete the label for this group.

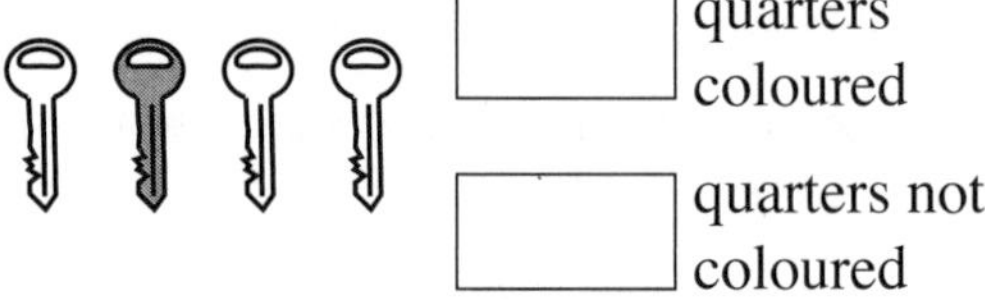


7. Write $0.80 in words.

8. In this hundred square, colour the fraction shown.
10 hundredths

9. Circle the numbers that round off to 200.
142, 189, 94, 100, 205

10. Eric recorded how many children wanted to play their favourite sport. How many chose Tennis?

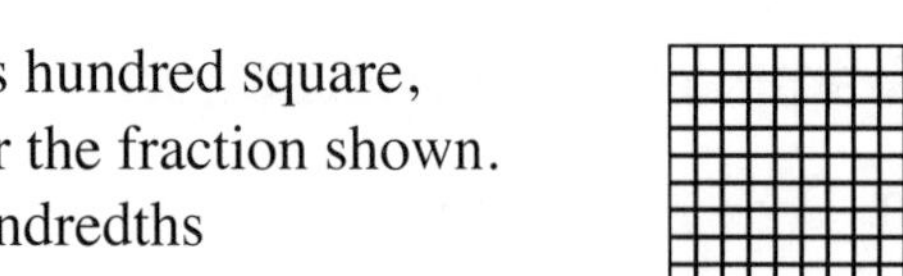


## Measurement and Geometry

11. Record the time you did these activities this morning.
(a) arrived at school
(b) finished morning tea
(c) started Maths

12. Colour the mass needed to balance the food item.

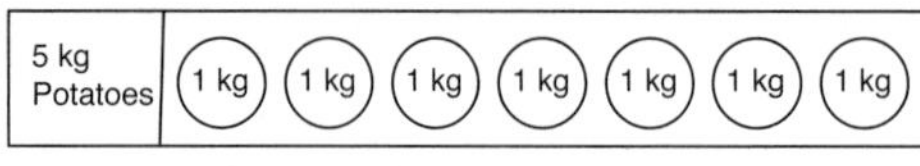


13. 1 m × 1 m =

14. $\frac{1}{2}$ L = _ _ _ _ a litre

15. Circle the lowest temperature.
18°C, 43°C, 63°C, 85°C, 36°C

16. Use a pencil and ruler to draw a trapezium.

17. Draw and name the cross-section of this shape.

18. This is a _ _ _ _ _ _ _ _ angle.

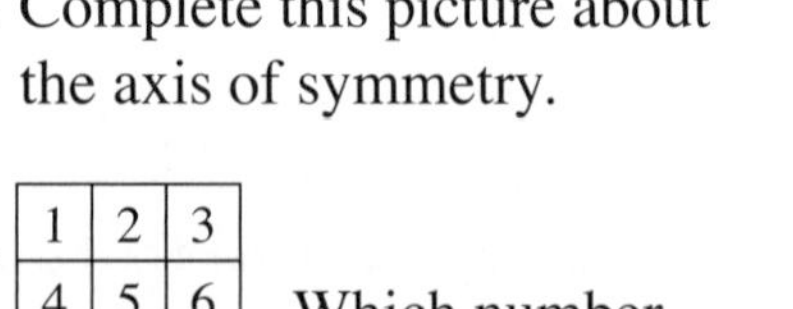

19. Complete this picture about the axis of symmetry.

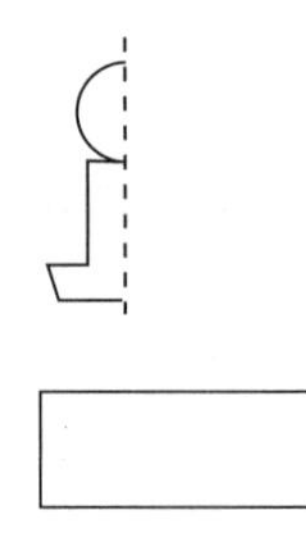

20.

| 1 | 2 | 3 |
|---|---|---|
| 4 | 5 | 6 |
| 7 | 8 | 9 |

Which number is below 6?

## Statistics and Probability

21. Seven trees were planted in a row. A flower sat in each space. How many flowers altogether?

## The Boy Who Cried Wolf

Peter was a young shepherd boy. His job was to watch over the sheep while they ate grass. He liked his job, but sometimes it was a bit boring. So one day he decided to play a joke on the nearby villagers. "Wolf! Help me—somebody help me!" he shouted loudly. Hearing the shepherd boy's cry, the villagers ran to assist Peter. When they arrived they saw no wolf. Peter would just stand there and laugh. "I fooled you all. Ha! Ha!" he giggled.

The villagers thought this was a very silly joke.

The next day, Peter played the same trick. "Help me! Wolf! Wolf!" he shouted again. Once again, the people of the village came running only to find the shepherd boy laughing. The third day, a hungry wolf really did come down the grassy hills with the idea of finding some fat, juicy sheep to munch on. "Wolf! Wolf!" screamed Peter. This time no villagers came to help him.

"He's only joking again. Let's ignore his cries for help," they said.

Moral: If you deceive people, they won't believe you when you are telling the truth.

## Reading and Comprehension

**1.** Peter yelled "Wolf" the first time because
(a) he was singing.
(b) the villagers couldn't hear him.
(c) he was good at cracking jokes.
(d) he was feeling bored.

**2.** What was the wolf after?
(a) Peter
(b) villagers
(c) grass
(d) sheep

**3.** How many times did Peter cry for help before the villagers ignored him?
(a) 1 (b) 2
(c) 3 (d) 4

**4.** What is a fable?

______________________________

**5.** Number these sentences in order (1–4).
(a) He decided to play a silly joke.
(b) He's probably only joking again.
(c) The villagers came running to his rescue.
(d) Peter was a young shepherd boy.

## Spelling and Vocabulary

Rewrite the misspelt words.

**6.** I'm often asked if I'm levle-headed!

______________________________

**7.** The crystal varse slipped off the kitchen bench. ______________

Circle the word that has the nearest meaning to the underlined word.

**8.** Five o'clock <u>suits</u> Nanna perfectly.
(a) fits (b) pleases
(c) serves (d) lovely

**9.** The girl <u>speared</u> the fish in the water.
(a) caught (b) stabbed
(c) stole (d) tool

Circle the correct word in brackets.

**10.** The Salvation Army is a good (course, cause).

**11.** The (cheif, chief) thing in a baby's life is love.

**12.** The policeman had (charged, charge) the man with stealing.

## Grammar and Punctuation

**13.** Underline the **adverbs** in these sentences.

"Come on quickly," Mum yelled. "Dinner is finally ready kids." I walked to the table slowly because I hate eating tripe.

**14.** Punctuate and capitalise this sentence.

we received an anonymous phone call on thursday evening

______________________________

______________________________

## Number and Algebra

1.

| + | 7 | 9 | 5 | 11 | 2 | 20 |
|---|---|---|---|---|---|---|
| 6 | | | | | | |

2.

| − | 6 | 7 | 8 | 9 | 10 | 20 |
|---|---|---|---|---|---|---|
| 6 | | | | | | |

3.

| × | 7 | 6 | 5 | 4 | 3 | 11 |
|---|---|---|---|---|---|---|
| 6 | | | | | | |

4. Write the number shown on the abacus. H T U

5. Complete this number sequence.

650, 649, 648, ___, ___, ___, ___, ___

6. Colour three sevenths of these hamburgers.

7. Write in decimal form: 95 cents.

8. Match the ones that are the same.

75 hundredths — 0.49
49 hundredths — 0.75
68 hundredths — 0.68

9. Is 2946 closer to 2900 or 3000?

10. Fill in the blank paths.

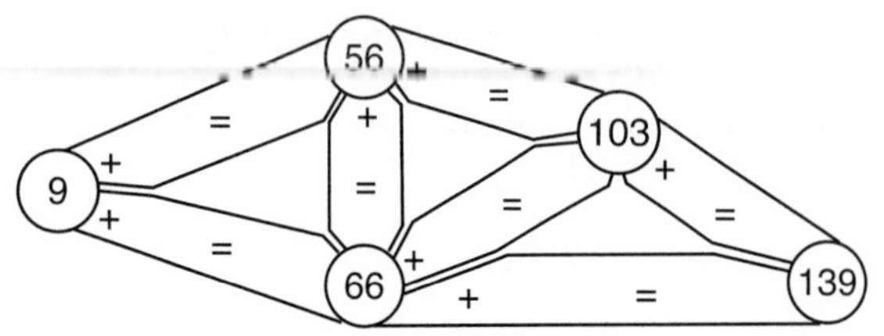


## Measurement and Geometry

11. Tick the right box. Time taken to brush your teeth. ☐ seconds ☐ minutes

12. Carrots cost $1/kg. How much for 5 kg of carrots?

13. $m^2$ means _ _ _ _ _ _ _ _ _ metre.

14. 9 litres − $\frac{1}{2}$ L = ___ L

15. What is roughly the average classroom temperature?

16. How many axes of symmetry does this polygon have?

17. Draw and name the cross-section of this shape.

18. How many arms does an angle have?

19. Draw in the axes of symmetry in these letters.

(a)

(b)

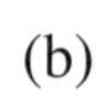

20.

| G | H | I |
|---|---|---|
| F | E | D |
| A | B | C |

Which letter is above C?

## Statistics and Probability

21.

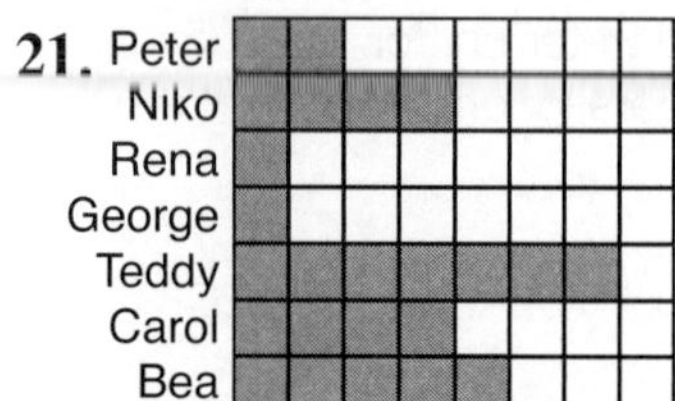


Who made the most number of phone calls last week?

## Brachiosaurus

Brachiosaurus was one of the sauropod group of dinosaurs, the largest creatures ever to walk on dry land. *Sauropoda* means 'lizard feet'; they had five toes, like lizards. These dinosaurs had tiny brains.

Brachiosaurus was a gigantic animal. Not only was it heavy, it was also very long and tall. It looked rather like a huge giraffe. Its neck was long, but its head was not much larger than a horse's head. The large reptile had thick, strong legs which looked like the legs of an enormous elephant.

Brachiosaurus lived over 65 million years ago. Its remains have been found in North America and Africa. It lived in forests and woods, often near lakes.

With such a long neck, this large beast was able to eat the leaves from tall trees, much like a giraffe. It may have been able to go into the water in search of food.

Brachiosaurus probably protected itself by crushing its attackers with its weight, or lashing them with its long, thick tail. In spite of its huge size, this plant-eating dinosaur was probably a fairly slow, peaceful animal.

From *Great Dinosaurs* by Ross Latham & Peter Sloan

## Reading and Comprehension

1. *Sauropoda* means
   (a) 'tiny brains'. (b) 'lizard feet'.
   (c) 'huge giraffe'. (d) 'horned animals'.

2. Brachiosaurs were
   (a) meat-eaters. (b) plant-eaters.
   (c) water creatures only. (d) running lizards.

3. The legs of the brachiosaurus resembled which other animal?
   (a) giraffe (b) elephant
   (c) horse (d) lizard

4. Find the adjective in the story which means 'placid'. ____________________

5. Number these sentences in order (1–4).
   (a) They were fairly slow animals.
   (b) Remains have been found in North America and Africa.
   (c) Brachiosaurs had tiny brains.
   (d) Their feet had five toes, like lizards.

## Spelling and Vocabulary

Rewrite the misspelt words.

6. For our last hollidays, we went to Hervey Bay.

   ____________________

7. The seal jumped threw the plastic hoop.

   ____________________

Circle the word that has the nearest meaning to the underlined word.

8. The ambulance <u>lost</u> no time in reaching the Childrens' Hospital.
   (a) loose (b) found
   (c) needed (d) wasted

9. The <u>branch</u> of the bank Dad belongs to is North Manly.
   (a) section (b) twig (c) part (d) team

Circle the correct word in brackets.

10. The students were in the (caring, care) of a kind teacher.

11. Mum placed the hot dish on the bench (careful, carefully).

12. My brother was instructed to complete a First Aid (course, cause).

## Grammar and Punctuation

13. Underline the **prepositions** in these sentences.

    Move the needle over and under, all the way to the end of the hessian. Tie off the threads before cutting them.

14. Punctuate and capitalise this sentence.

    dr julie smithers is our local gp

    ____________________

    ____________________

# Mathematics

UNIT 7

## Number and Algebra

1.

| + | 8 | 9 | 3 | 5 | 11 | 17 |
|---|---|---|---|---|---|---|
| 7 | | | | | | |

2.

| – | 8 | 15 | 17 | 12 | 19 | 27 |
|---|---|---|---|---|---|---|
| 7 | | | | | | |

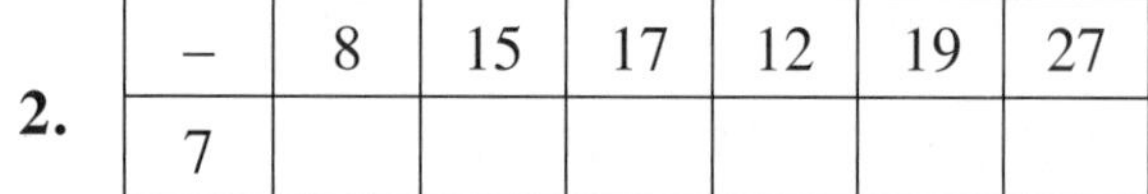

3.

| ÷ | 14 | 28 | 7 | 0 | 35 | 77 |
|---|---|---|---|---|---|---|
| 7 | | | | | | |

**4.** Write the number shown by the blocks.

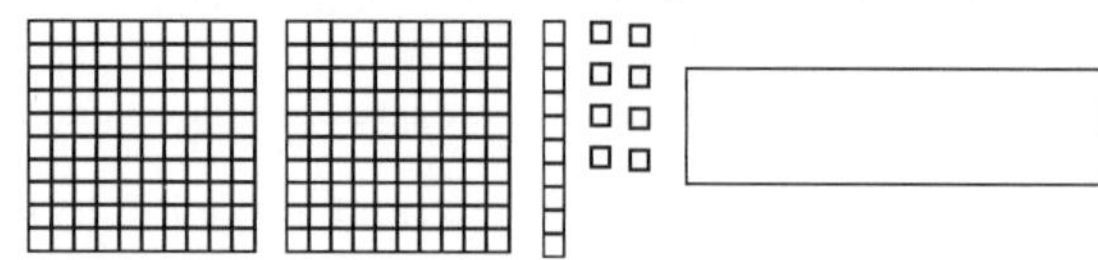

**5.** Finish the number sequence.

900, 800, 700, ☐, ☐, ☐,

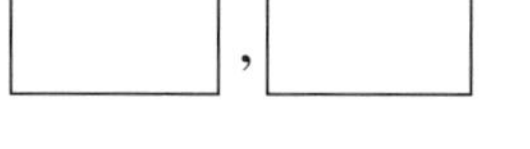

**6.** Shade the fraction given.
42 hundredths

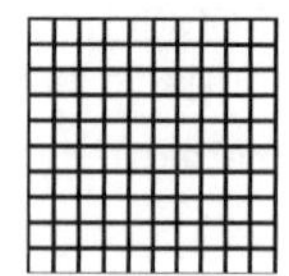

**7.** What must be added to this amount to get $2?

**8.** Write in decimal form:

(a) 1 and 77 hundredths

(b) 3 and 26 hundredths

(c) 1 and 50 hundredths

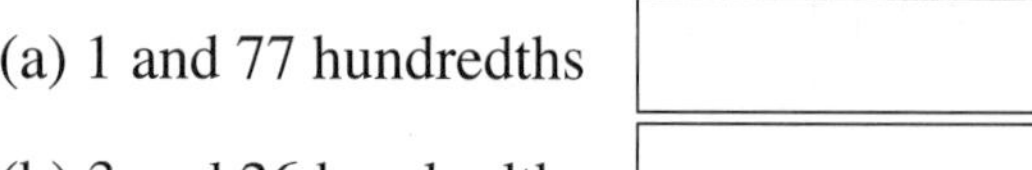

**9.** True or False?
1427 is rounded off to 2000.

**10.** Mrs Simms earns $15 an hour selling cosmetics. If she works for 4 hours each day from Monday to Thursday, how much does she earn in 4 days?

## Measurement and Geometry

**11.** How many days in September this year?

**12.** Measure the length of this set of blocks.

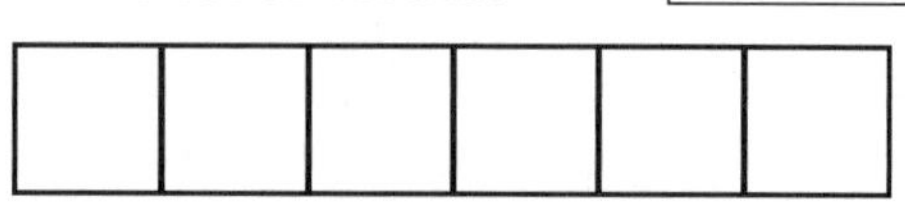

**13.** Circle the two little maths words found in the word k i l o g r a m.

**14.** Colour to the half-a-litre level on this container.

**15.** Write 82°C in words.

**16.** Circle the triangle which has no equal sides?

(a) (b) (c)

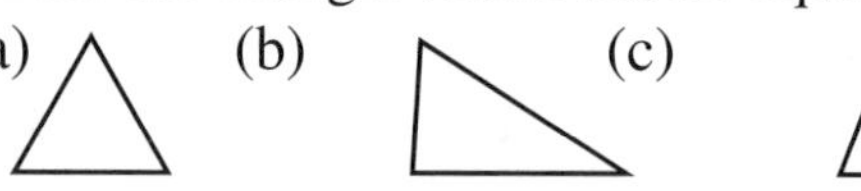

**17.** How many edges does a square pyramid have?

**18.** How many right angles will fit into a straight angle?

**19.** Complete this picture if the broken line is an axis of symmetry.

**20.**

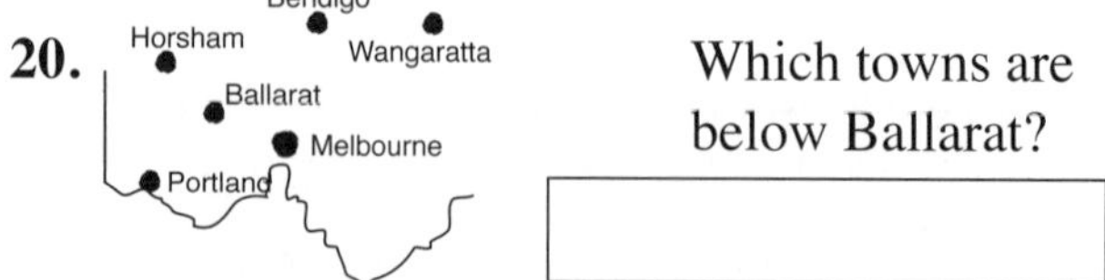


Which towns are below Ballarat?

## Statistics and Probability

**21.**

| A | B | D | B | F | G |
|---|---|---|---|---|---|
| X | Play the game | | | | A |
| B | A | L | K | C | B |

Which letter is the most popular?

## Ho! Ho! Ho!

A week before Christmas, on a wintry night,
Snow lay around like a blanket of white.
The air was bitter, colder than ice
And no one went out without thinking twice.
Then all of a sudden a voice thundered out
Piercing the silence that lay all about.
It shouted so loud, so sharp and so clear,
That voice was meant for the whole world to hear.

Booming from somewhere up in the North Pole,
The voice said: "My pants have sprung a
  huge hole!
Look at the back of me! See the big tear!
You could park a gigantic battleship there!
It's against the law—a crime, do you hear?—
For a chap like me to expose his rear!
How can I possibly go, 'Ho, ho, ho!'
With my underpants all out on show?"

Then Santa himself appeared at the door,
Hands covering the rip, which tore a bit more.
With forehead so wrinkled and face so cross,
He spluttered, "Is this how you treat your boss?
One of you elves must be playing a joke—
A mighty mean thing to do to a bloke!
This can't be the same suit I wore last year,
When spreading around all that Christmas cheer."

From *Ho, Ho, Ho!* by Jan Weeks

### Reading and Comprehension

1. What was *like a blanket of white*?
   (a) Santa's underpants (b) the snow
   (c) the ice (d) Santa's beard

2. The word in the poem which means 'reveal' is
   (a) rear. (b) expose.
   (c) hide. (d) spreading.

3. In the poem, which word rhymes with *joke*?
   (a) pants (b) coke
   (c) huge (d) awake

4. What disturbed the silence on that cold wintry night?

   ______________________________

5. Number these sentences in order (1–4).
   (a) Santa's pants had sprung a hole.
   (b) His face was cross and wrinkled.
   (c) It was the week before Christmas.
   (d) Then Santa appeared at the door.

### Spelling and Vocabulary

Rewrite the misspelt words.

6. William adores eating raspberries with kream.

   ______________________________

7. He got the suprise of his life when the teacher appeared.

   ______________________________

Circle the word that has the nearest meaning to the underlined word.

8. Try not to <u>worry</u> about your English test on Friday.
   (a) fret (b) trouble
   (c) wish (d) whisper

9. The <u>worth</u> of the necklace is over five thousand dollars.
   (a) expense (b) price
   (c) worse (d) change

Circle the correct word in brackets.

10. (Merry, Marry) Christmas everyone!

11. I saw the car crash into the pylon (meself, myself, myselves).

12. (Sore, Saw) the pinewood into three equal pieces.

### Grammar and Punctuation

13. Underline the **nouns** in these sentences.

    Comets are small pieces of rock and ice that orbit the Sun in an oval path. Sometimes they come very close to the Sun.

14. Punctuate and capitalise this sentence.

    many of the prizes won by the athletes were still in the principals office

    ______________________________

    ______________________________

## Number and Algebra

1. Follow this addition path.

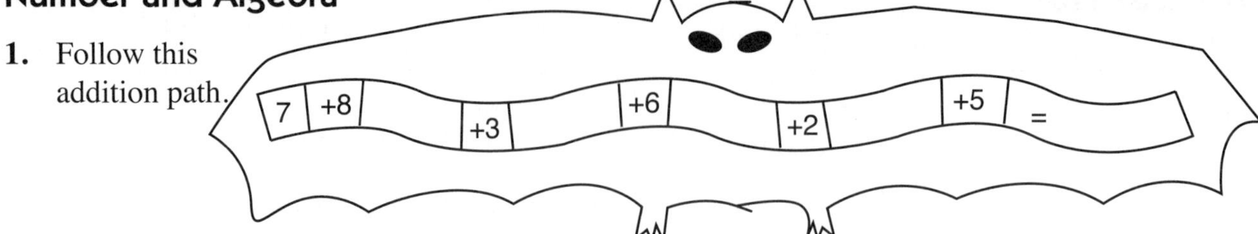


2. Follow this subtraction path.

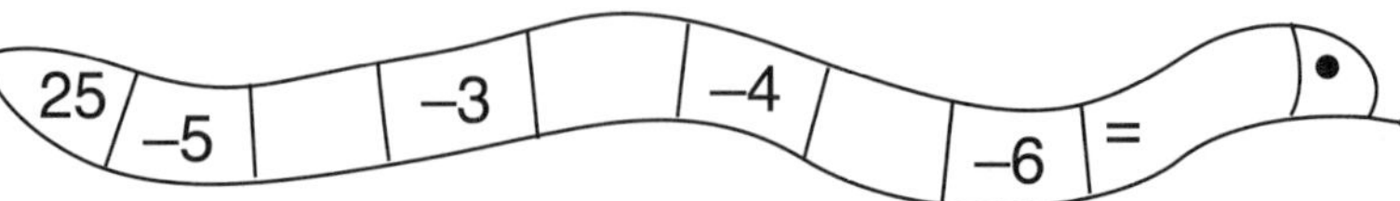


3. Complete these division wheels. (a)

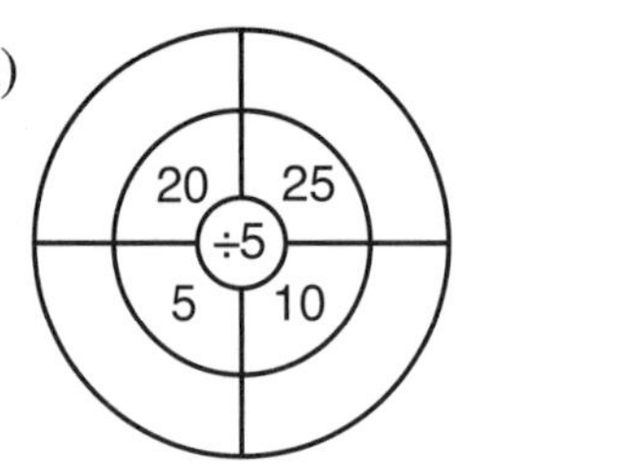


(b)

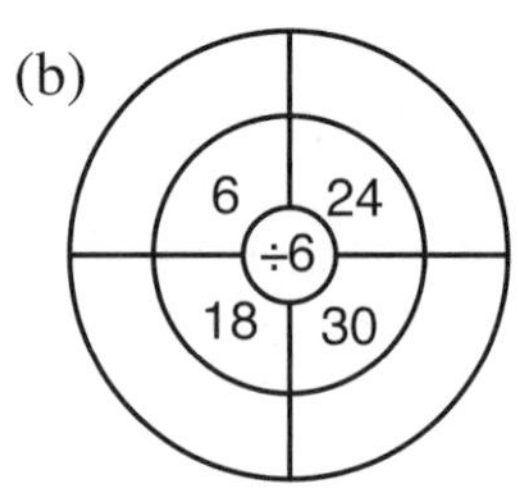


4. Circle the tens digit in 4518.

5. Complete this sequence: 9643, 9644, 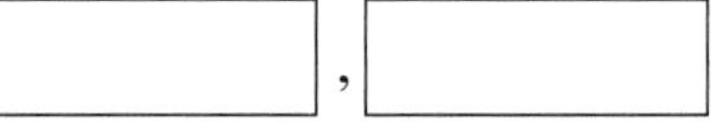 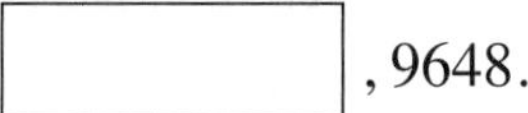 , 9648.

6. Shade nine and a half shoes.

7. Check out these coins. What is the total?

8. Write in digit form:

(a) one and thirty-eight hundredths

(b) three and ninety-two hundredths

9. Estimate: (a) How long it takes you to get to school each morning.

(b) How many loaves of bread your family consumes in one week.

10. Thomas lives 300 metres from school. Ives lives about 500 metres away. How much further does Ives live?

## Measurement and Geometry

11. Circle the correct answer. A leap year has: 360 days, 366 days, 365 days, 356 days.

12. What is the total mass of these objects?

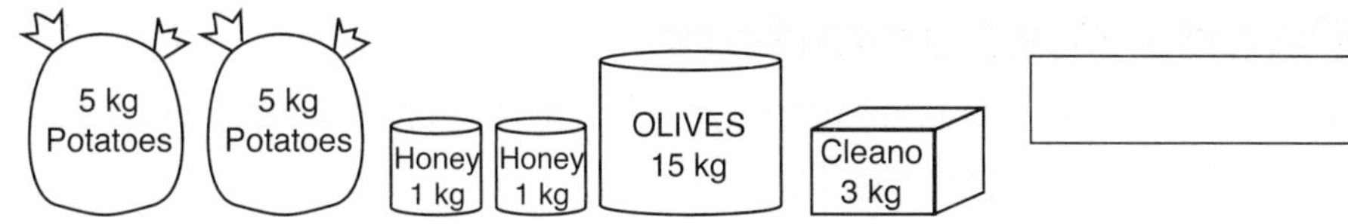


13. What is the area of this shape?

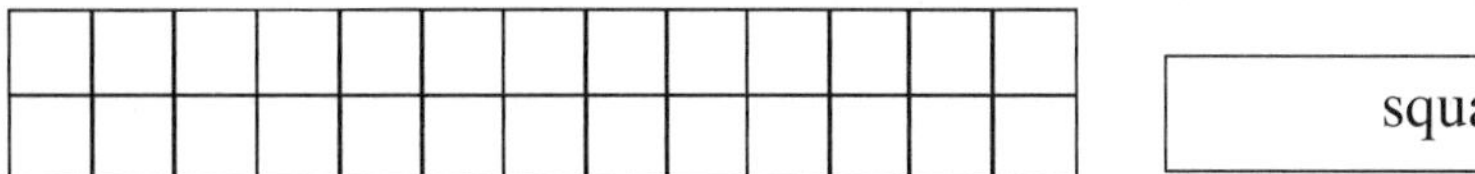

squares

14. What is the capacity of five bottles of juice, each containing five litres?

15. What temperature is shown on this thermometer?

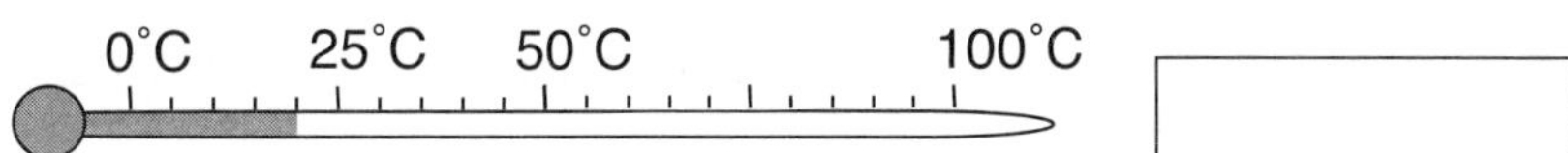


16. Which of these statements about rectangles is not true?

(a) Rectangles are heavy.
(b) The long side of a rectangle is called the length.
(c) All rectangles have a breadth.

17. Using five rectangles (the same size) and two equal pentagons, we can form the solid shape known as a ______.

18. Which angle is the sharpest ?

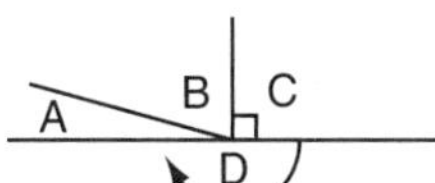


19. Draw in the line of symmetry.

20. F E D C B A / 1 2 3 4 5 6

The tick is at (2, B). Find the location of:

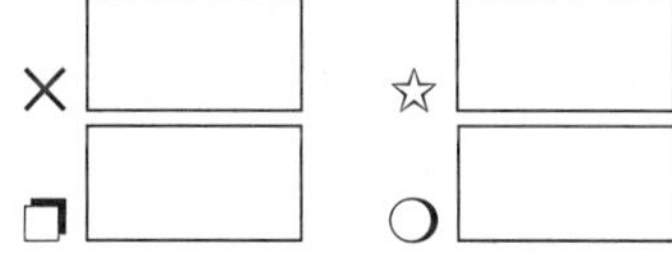

## Statistics and Probability

21. Body Mass

Kilograms: 0, 10, 20, 30, 40

KAY, BETH, NICK, TED, JAN

(a) Who has the greatest body mass?

(b) What is the total mass of the five kids?

## Panda Ambassadors

The Chinese Government lent Australia two giant pandas as a special Bicentennial gift. Xiao Xiao and Fei Fei visited zoos in Melbourne, Sydney and Auckland before returning home to China.

Fei Fei (say 'Fay Fay') was found, abandoned and starving, in 1986. She was six months old. Her Chinese name means 'the time of flowering', because she was found in springtime.

Xiao Xiao (say 'Jow Jow') wandered into a village during a storm. His name means 'shower from the sky' and it comes from the name of the village, Xiao Jia Wan.

Both pandas were taken to a panda reserve and looked after.

Fei Fei and Xiao Xiao are panda ambassadors, promoting the cause of conservation. They are working for the survival of their species. Although they are still too young to breed, their job will continue when they join in China's breeding program for pandas.

This breeding program, with international co-operation, is the panda's only hope for survival. If it fails, the giant panda will be extinct by the 21st century.

From *Pandas* by Christine Deacon

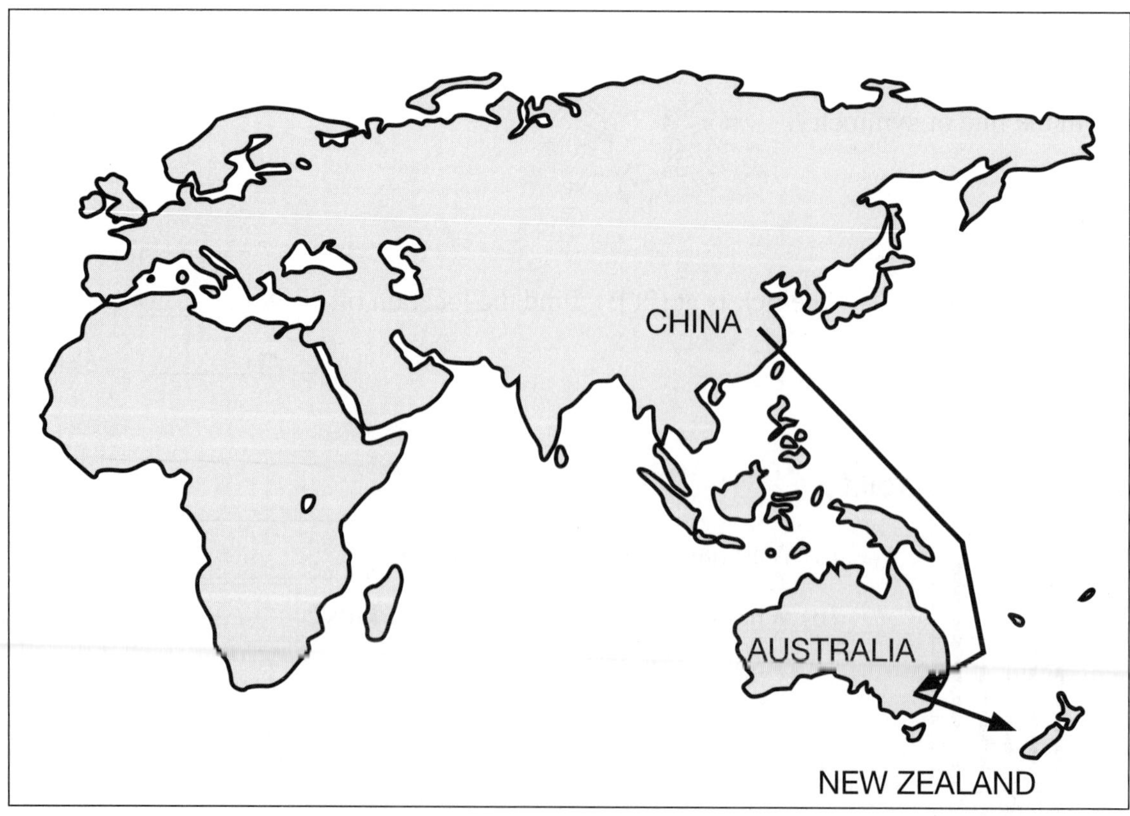

## Reading and Comprehension

1. Why were the pandas in Australia?
   (a) It's warmer here.
   (b) They became Australian Ambassadors.
   (c) They were on loan during our Bicentenary.
   (d) China had too many pandas.

2. Give the translation of the name *Xiao Xiao*.
   (a) time of flowering
   (b) Taronga Park
   (c) showering rain
   (d) shower from the sky

3. What is the Chinese Government's ultimate fear?
   (a) Australia will buy them.
   (b) Pandas may become extinct.
   (c) Auckland is too far.
   (d) Pandas don't know how to breed.

4. Which main cause do pandas represent?

   ______________________________

5. Number these sentences in order (1–4).
   (a) Fei Fei was found abandoned in 1986.
   (b) The pandas are too young to breed.
   (c) Xiao Xiao wandered into a village during a storm.
   (d) Australia was loaned two giant pandas.

## Spelling and Vocabulary

Rewrite these sentences, correcting the misspelt words.

6. The pandas are ambbasadors promoteing the cause of conversation.

   ______________________________

   ______________________________

7. Chinna is worried that the giant pander will be estinkt by the twenty-fist sentury.

   ______________________________

   ______________________________

Which word has the same or nearly the same meaning as the underlined word?

8. This breeding program is the panda's only chance for <u>survival</u>.
   (a) swimming (b) surveying
   (c) living (d) extinction

9. The <u>breeding</u> program will be achieved with international co-operation.
   (a) reproducing (b) dieback
   (c) bamboo (d) herbivorous

Circle the correct word in brackets.

10. The panda (reserve, reserves) is in the mountains.

11. The breeding program will (continue, continues) for many years.

12. Match the meanings with their correct glossary terms.

| | |
|---|---|
| (a) dieback | 1. ambassador |
| (b) official messenger | 2. tropical plant (grass-like) |
| (c) survival | 3. plant death |
| (d) bamboo | 4. no longer existing |
| (e) extinct | 5. in existence |
| (f) breeding | 6. having babies |

## Grammar and Punctuation

13. Underline the **nouns** in these sentences.

    The giant panda is a herbivorous, or plant-eating, mammal. Its bones are very heavy, making it about twice as heavy as you would expect for an animal of its size. Pandas, like humans, can grab things tightly with their hands because they have thumbs.

14. Punctuate and capitalise this sentence correctly.

    fei fei and xiao xiao were lent to australia as a special bicentennial gift

    ______________________________

    ______________________________

    ______________________________

## Number and Algebra

1.

| + | 7 | 0 | 9 | 6 | 2 | 25 |
|---|---|---|---|---|---|---|
| 9 | | | | | | |

2.

| – | 10 | 15 | 18 | 19 | 9 | 28 |
|---|---|---|---|---|---|---|
| 9 | | | | | | |

3.

| × | 1 | 5 | 9 | 3 | 10 | 11 |
|---|---|---|---|---|---|---|
| 9 | | | | | | |

4. Write the number for:
(a) 2000 + 400 + 30 + 3
(b) 7000 + 900 + 8

5. Complete the sequence.
1.96, 1.95, ___ , ___ , ___

6. Complete the labels to show the total parts coloured.

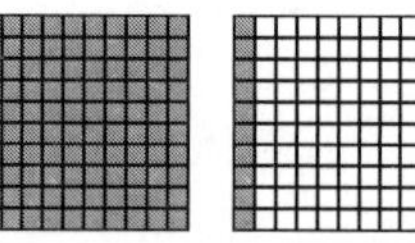

___ and ___ hundredths

7. $0.30, $0.45 Total = ___

8. Colour in these decimals.
(a) 0.8 (b) 0.6

9. Circle the best estimate: 20, 200, 10

10. Edward bought 6 extension cords, each 3.5 metres in length. What was the total length of the cords?

## Measurement and Geometry

11. Complete the labels for the time shown.

7 :
past

12. 1 metre 60 centimetres = ___ m ___ cm

13. Predict how many square metres your bedroom floor is.

14. Find four bathroom products that have liquid volume measurements.
1. ___ 2. ___
3. ___ 4. ___

15. What temperature is shown on this scale?

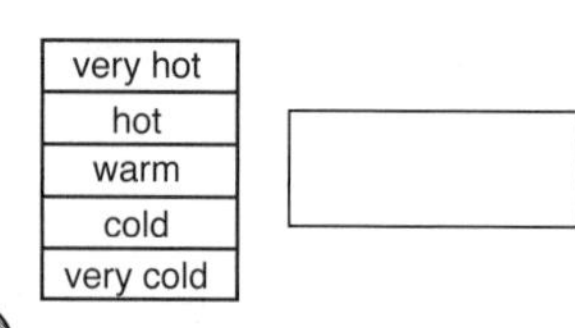


16. This shape is called an _ _ _ _

17. The shaded face is called the _ _ _ _

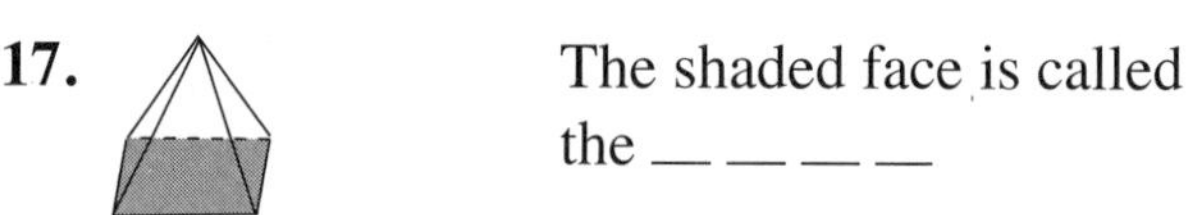

18. On each shape below, colour the horizontal lines red and the oblique lines blue.
(a) (b)

19. Draw in all the axes of symmetry for each diagram.
(a) (b)

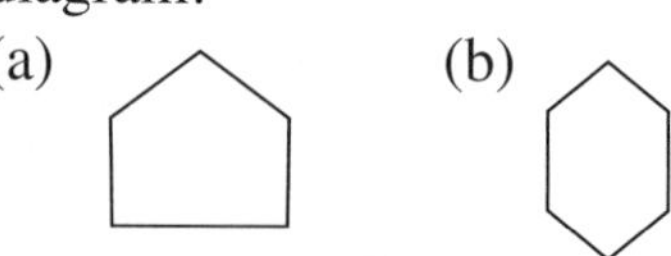

20. Draw a hat on the eighth child.

## Statistics and Probability

21. Mum bought 6 apples, 10 oranges and 7 pears. Complete the column graph to show this.

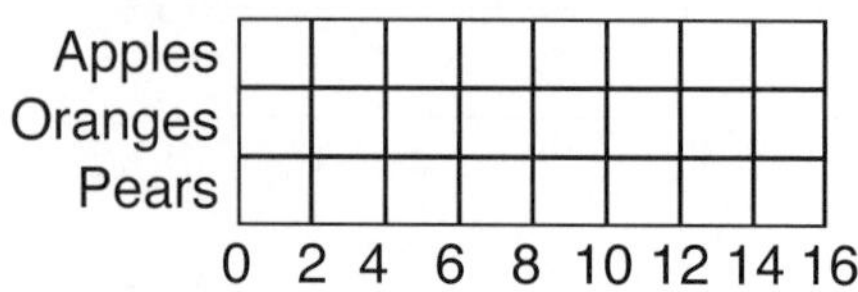

## Sp ... sp ... sp ... Spaghetti Bolognaise!!!

500 g (lean) minced beef
1 large onion (chopped)
$1\frac{1}{2}$ cups thick tomato puree
2 tablespoons tomato paste
2 tablespoons oil
salt, pepper, sugar, oregano
salted water
375 g spaghetti
grated cheese

1. Heat oil in pan. Add beef, onion. Cook gently. Stir frequently until meat is well browned.
2. Add tomato puree and tomato paste and cook over very low heat for about 20–25 minutes; add seasoning to taste.
3. Cook spaghetti in salted boiling water. Drain and add oregano.
4. Place spaghetti into large bowl and top with bolognaise sauce.
5. Serve hot with cheese if desired. Serves about 6.

## Reading and Comprehension

1. The second instruction in this recipe is to
   (a) heat the oil. (b) add the tomato paste.
   (c) stir frequently. (d) add the beef and onion.

2. Oregano is a
   (a) type of mince.
   (b) Italian meal.
   (c) member of the orange family.
   (d) type of herb.

3. This recipe caters for
   (a) 5. (b) 2. (c) 500 g. (d) 6.

4. Is 375 g (of spaghetti) more or less than half a kilo? ____________

5. Number these sentences in order (1–4).
   (a) Cook the beef gently.
   (b) Place spaghetti in a bowl.
   (c) Serve hot with cheese.
   (d) Add the tomato paste.

## Spelling and Vocabulary

Rewrite the misspelt words.

6. The doctor will eggzamin the patient and then prescribe some medicine.

   ____________

7. I don't expect the vizita to arrive before seven o'clock.

   ____________

Circle the word that has the nearest meaning to the underlined word.

8. <u>Still</u>, there's nothing we can do about it now Johnny.
   (a) nevertheless
   (b) suddenly
   (c) but
   (d) so

9. The flower was <u>stripped</u> of all its petals.
   (a) dressed
   (b) covered
   (c) protected
   (d) bare

Circle the correct word in brackets.

10. Maria had to walk on stage to (except, accept) her netball trophy.

11. (You'll, Ule) be late for dinner if you don't get moving!

12. The rock star (wrote, written) his autograph in red pen.

## Grammar and Punctuation

13. Underline the **nouns** in these sentences.

    On the distant hill, there was a small cottage. It was a pretty scene as white smoke was floating out of its chimney.

14. Punctuate and capitalise this sentence.

    the little children were sent outside to play with the hose

    ____________

    ____________

# Mathematics



## Number and Algebra

1.

| + | 6 | 9 | 10 | 3 | 8 | 26 |
|---|---|---|---|---|---|---|
| 5 | | | | | | |

2.

| – | 10 | 15 | 5 | 7 | 9 | 34 |
|---|---|---|---|---|---|---|
| 5 | | | | | | |

3.

| ÷ | 5 | 50 | 20 | 40 | 25 | 100 |
|---|---|---|---|---|---|---|
| 5 | | | | | | |

4. Write the place value of each bold digit.

(a) 321**7** (b) 93**6**5

(c) **3**465

5. Complete this sequence: 1.77, 1.78, 1.79, , ,

6. Shade in 0.54

7. pen .............$0.50
pencil .........$0.25 Total cost ..

8. True or False?
0.29 =

9. True or False?
An egg weighs about 2 kg.

10. Which number is a multiple of 3, is less than 30 and has a five in the ones place?

## Measurement and Geometry

11. Write the time that is one minute before:

(a) 10:54 (b) 6:00

12. Write these in centimetres.

(a) 1 m 25 cm =

(b) 3 m 40 cm =

13. Circle the one that is less than one square metre:
top of a matchbox, classroom floor, chalkboard

14. Selby has ten two-litre bottles of kitchen detergent. What is the overall volume?

15. Which scale shows an orange reading?

(a) (b)

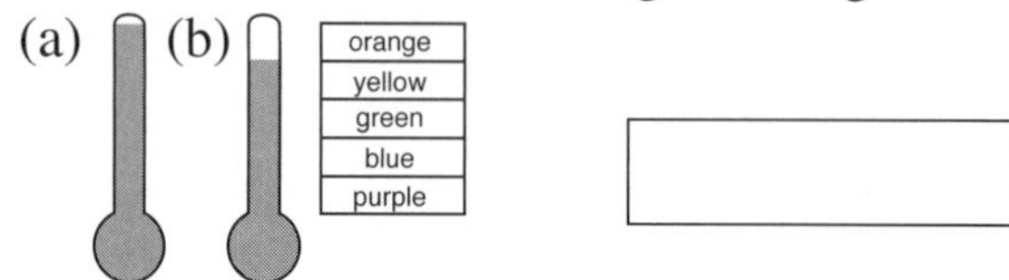


16. Both of these shapes are r _ _ _ _ _ _ _ .

17. an e _ _ _

18. Circle the one that shows parallel lines.

(a) (b) (c) (d)

19. Complete this picture using the axis of symmetry.

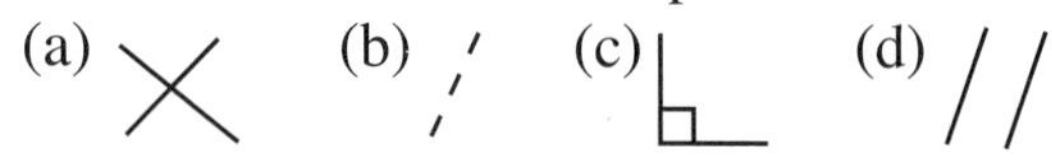

20. Draw a picture of a chair from the side view.

## Statistics and Probability

21.

| Books read by Tom<br>▢ stands for 20 books | |
|---|---|
| 2009 | ▢ ▢ ▢ |
| 2010 | ▢ ▢ |
| 2011 | ▢ ▢ ▢ ▢ |
| 2012 | ▢ |

How many books did Tom read in 2011?

## Carpet Cleaning

1.

**AFFORDABLE**
**Carpet Cleaning & Pest Control**
Carpet cleaning from **$10**
Pest Control at Discount Prices
• Lower Rates Apply for EMPTY homes
• Lounge Suite & Car Uphol. Cleaning & Stain Protection
Local Owner 3268 7000

2.

**CC PP TT CLEANING**
**From Only $9 per Room**
3222 333
ALL SUBURBS
Same Day Service Guaranteed

3.

5 Rooms plus Hall Steam Cleaned with an Int. or Ext. Pest control for only $160
**All Work Guaranteed**
Phone 015 666 777

4.

Floor Clean. & Maintenance Service
**5 Rooms for $49** + Hallway Free
**Pest Control & Carpet Clean. $75**
Free Call 1 800 888 888

## Reading and Comprehension

**1.** Ad 2 tells you that all your carpets can be cleaned
(a) for $9. (b) for under $9.
(c) for more than $9. (d) from $9.

**2.** If your lounge suite was badly stained it would be best to refer to
(a) ad 1. (b) ad 2.
(c) ad 3. (d) ad 4.

**3.** Which of the ads doesn't mention pest control?
(a) ad 1 (b) ad 2
(c) ad 3 (d) ad 4

**4.** What do these abbreviations stand for?
(a) int. ____________________
(b) ext. ____________________

**5.** Number these words in alphabetical order (1–6).
(a) cleaning (b) deluxe
(c) service (d) pest
(e) guaranteed (f) carpet

## Spelling and Vocabulary

Rewrite the misspelt words.

**6.** The kitchen stofe had a ceramic glass top.

____________________

**7.** Give the kitchen a good sweap will you Sue?

____________________

Circle the word that has the nearest meaning to the underlined word.

**8.** Some people believe America is a very <u>strong</u> nation.
(a) delicate (b) powerful
(c) spread (d) insipid

**9.** The ranger had to <u>shift</u> the mud from the car's wheels.
(a) settle (b) preserve
(c) sink (d) move

Circle the correct word in brackets.

**10.** Try not to saw the (would, wood) against the grain.

**11.** She gave a detailed account of what she (saw, sore).

**12.** The new Year 4 teacher is (male, mail).

## Grammar and Punctuation

**13.** Underline the **prepositions** in these sentences.

That's a silly spot for it. Put the vase on the side-table near my bed. Don't forget the tulips!

**14.** Punctuate and capitalise this sentence.

tim the german shepherd waited for his master near the old rusty gate

____________________

____________________

## Number and Algebra

1.

| + | 1 | 2 | 3 | 4 | 5 | 17 |
|---|---|---|---|---|---|---|
| 7 | | | | | | |

2.

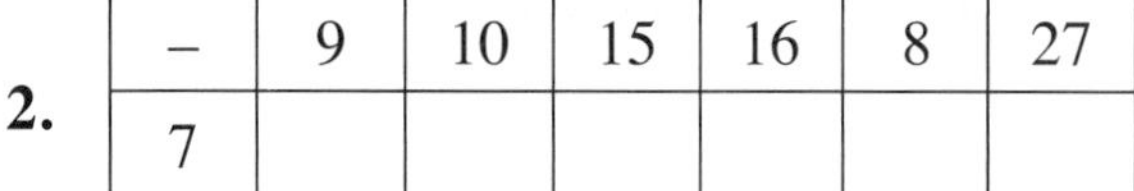

| – | 9 | 10 | 15 | 16 | 8 | 27 |
|---|---|---|---|---|---|---|
| 7 | | | | | | |

3.

| × | 2 | 5 | 1 | 7 | 9 | 21 |
|---|---|---|---|---|---|---|
| 7 | | | | | | |

4. Write the number shown on the abacus

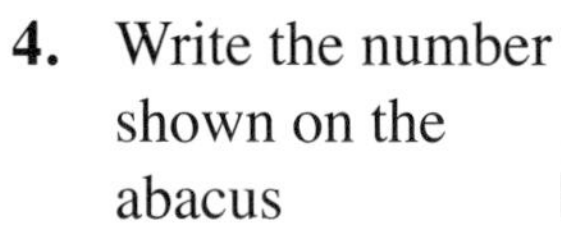

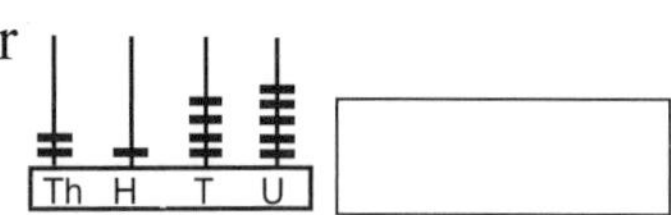


5. Fill in the spaces.

7800, 7700, ____ , ____ , ____

6. Colour twenty-eight hundredths.

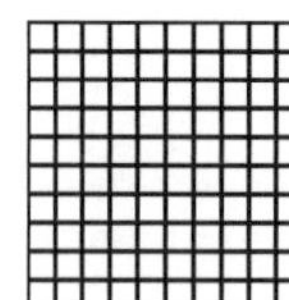

7. How much are three carrots?

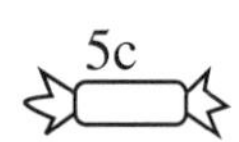

8. Write in decimal form:

(a) 1 and 37 hundredths

(b) 2 and 20 hundredths

9. True or False?
A truck is about 2 metres long.

10. Use your calculator to complete this pattern of subtracting 13: 149, 136,

## Measurement and Geometry

11. Complete the label for the time shown.

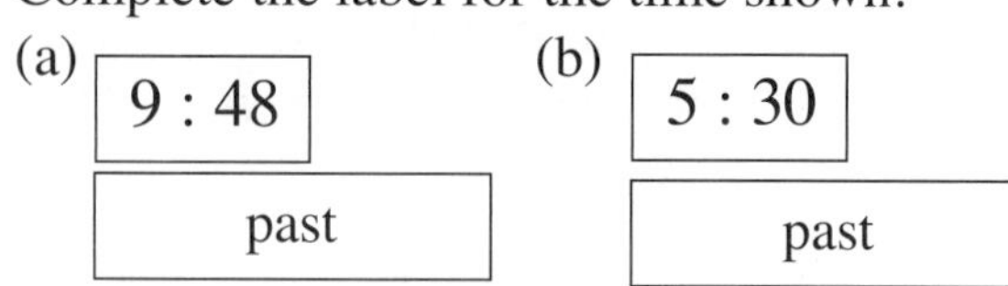


12. Write these as m and cm.

(a) 1.70 m (b) 4.58 m

13. Circle the one that is more than a square metre.
top of a chalk box, corridor floor, cover of a book

14. If a bottle of food colouring holds a tenth of a litre, how many bottles are needed to fill a one-litre container?

15. Show the 'red' level on Lee's thermometer.

16. How many sides does a trapezium have?

17. Complete the set of pictures for this solid.

| Top | Front | Side |
|---|---|---|
| | | |

18. Tick the correct statement.
This polygon has:

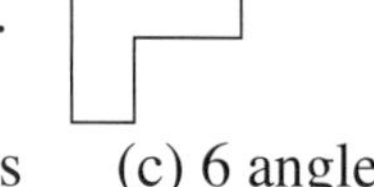

(a) 5 sides (b) 7 vertices (c) 6 angles

19. How many axes of symmetry does this shape have?

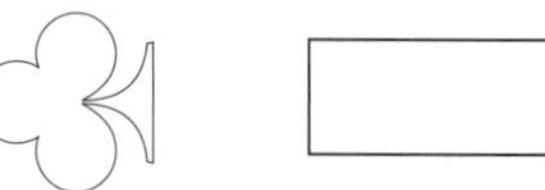

20. Circle the colour which is to the left of blue.

| red | blue |
|---|---|
| green | purple |
| orange | yellow |

## Statistics and Probability

21. JULY ~~||||~~ ~~||||~~ ~~||||~~ ~~||||~~ ~~||||~~ ~~||||~~ ~~||||~~ ~~||||~~ ~~||||~~ ~~||||~~ ~~||||~~ ~~||||~~ ~~||||~~ ~~||||~~ ~~||||~~ ~~||||~~ ~~||||~~ ~~||||~~ ~~||||~~ ~~||||~~ ~~||||~~ ~~||||~~ ||||

How many calls did Harold make in July?

## Legend: Why the Numbat Has a Red Back

Perentie the goanna and Walpurti the numbat were camping together in the desert.

They decided to paint pictures on each other's backs.

Walpurti took a stick and painted rings on Perentie's skin. Perentie painted stripes on Walpurti's fur.

Perentie was very pleased with the circles on his back, but Walpurti was furious when he saw the stripes Perentie had given him.

Walpurti picked up some red sand and threw it over his back.

The sand left a bright red blaze across the stripes.

That is why the numbat has a rusty red blaze on its back, as well as stripes.

From *Numbat, Run!* by Jill Morris & Lynne Tracey

## Reading and Comprehension

1. Which animal threw the red sand?
   (a) goanna (b) numbat
   (c) lizard (d) redback spider

2. Walpurti was furious. This means he was
   (a) glad. (b) calm.
   (c) enraged. (d) happy.

3. What did the animals use to paint with?
   (a) toothbrush
   (b) twig
   (c) the leaf of a native plant
   (d) their tails

4. What is a *legend*?

   ______________________________

   ______________________________

5. Number these sentences in order (1–4).
   (a) Perentie painted stripes.
   (b) Walpurti was furious.
   (c) The animals were camping.
   (d) Walpurti painted rings.

## Spelling and Vocabulary

Rewrite the misspelt words.

6. The gardener will speek on native plants today.

   ______________________________

7. This large spune is known as a soup ladle.

   ______________________________

Circle the word that has the nearest meaning to the underlined word.

8. Dad <u>stole</u> into the baby's room.
   (a) screamed
   (b) pounded
   (c) skipped
   (d) crept

9. Gold has been <u>struck</u> in the inner areas of Melbourne.
   (a) raised
   (b) steady
   (c) found
   (d) fixed

Circle the correct word in brackets.

10. My (speach, speech) had to be about three minutes long.

11. In her (spear, spare) time, Meredith reads a lot.

12. The (fith, fifth) child in the tuckshop queue was wearing gumboots.

## Grammar and Punctuation

13. Underline the **nouns** in these sentences.

    The hen in the wooden box laid a golden egg. Mr Brown picked it up and placed it neatly in his woollen pocket.

14. Punctuate and capitalise this sentence.

    i went to the brisbane library to borrow quest against time but someone had already taken it out

    ______________________________

    ______________________________

    ______________________________

## Number and Algebra

1.

| + | 6 | 7 | 8 | 9 | 10 | 26 |
|---|---|---|---|---|---|---|
| 6 | | | | | | |

2.

| – | 16 | 15 | 14 | 13 | 12 | 27 |
|---|---|---|---|---|---|---|
| 6 | | | | | | |

3.

| × | 10 | 9 | 8 | 7 | 6 | 20 |
|---|---|---|---|---|---|---|
| 6 | | | | | | |

4. Write 4702 in expanded notation.

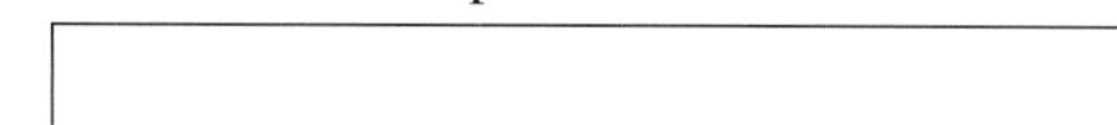

5. Complete: 9000, 8000, 7000,

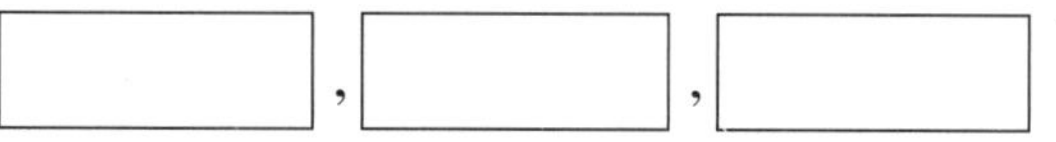

6. Colour the fraction given and then complete the label: 72 hundredths

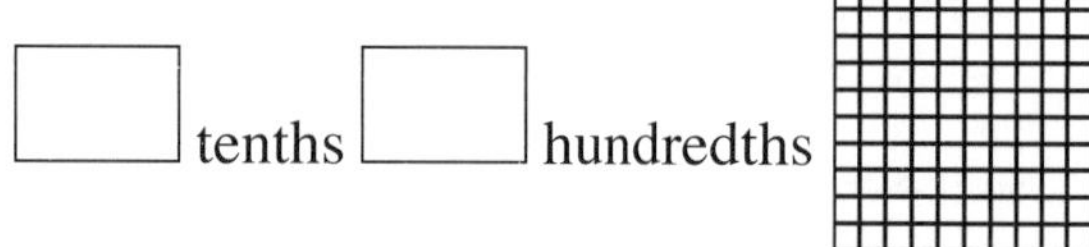


7. How many \$5 notes have the same value as \$30?

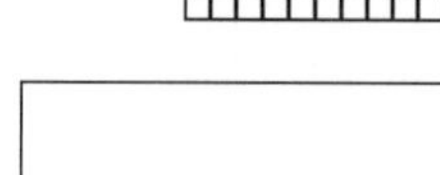

8. Complete this label.

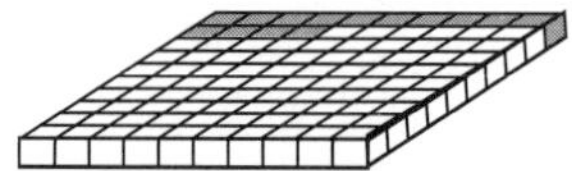

| Ones | • | Tenths | Hundredths |
|---|---|---|---|
| 0 | • | | |

9. The alphabet has one thousand, twenty-six or eighty letters? Circle the correct one.

10. How many triangles can you see altogether in this diagram? (watch out for overlaps)

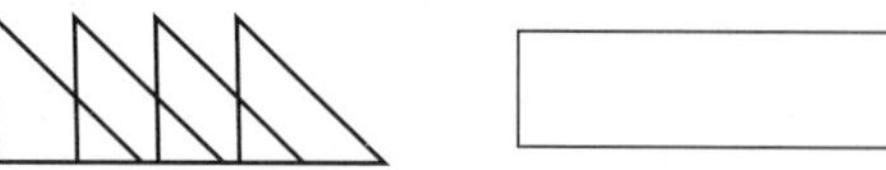

## Measurement and Geometry

11. (a) How many days in a year?
(b) How many days in a leap year?

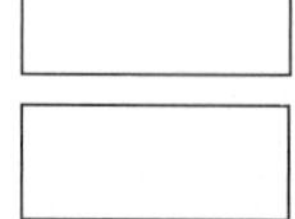

12. Write these measurements in decimal form.

(a) 1 m 25 cm

(b) 9 m 12 cm

13. Name two things in your room that would have a surface area of about 1 $m^2$.

1.

2.

14. 220 L – 100 L = ☐ L

15. What is the freezing point of water?

16. Circle the rigid model.

(a)

(b)

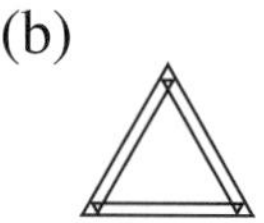

17. Each of these cross-sections will be a:

18. Shade in red all the angles in this shape.

19. Draw in the axis of symmetry.

20. Draw 3 rows of 12 eggs.

## Statistics and Probability

21. Balloons blown up

30
20
10
0
Anne Jan Jill Sam Tim Don

How many balloons were blown up altogether?

## New Arrivals

Jeanette Lynn was born at the Royal Womens' Hospital on August 10, weighing in at 2590 g (5 lb 6 oz). Jeanette is the third child and second daughter of Mt Marney couple Rigby and Lucy Lexine.

Greta Nydia Margen was born at the Logan Hospital on August 11, weighing 3045 g (6 lb 10 oz). Greta is the first child of Nicholas and Susan Ada from Upper Mt Gravatt.

## Reading and Comprehension

1. Who is Nicholas?
   (a) the father of Jeanette
   (b) the doctor who delivered the babies
   (c) the son of Greta
   (d) Greta's dad

2. 3045 g is about
   (a) 3 kg. (b) 4 kg.
   (c) 3.5 kg. (d) 5 kg.

3. Jeanette's mum's name is
   (a) Lynn.
   (b) Rigby.
   (c) Lexine.
   (d) Lucy.

4. Name the couple who have two other children.

   ______________________________

5. Number these masses in ascending order (1–5).
   (a) 3045 g (b) 3054 g
   (c) 2590 g (d) 2950 g
   (e) 3000 g

## Spelling and Vocabulary

Rewrite the misspelt words.

6. Just for now, this crate will serv as a chair.

   ______________________________

7. The bushfire, last Wednesday, caused a bit of a stirr.

   ______________________________

Circle the word that has the nearest meaning to the underlined word.

8. The artist <u>shaped</u> the clay into the form of a tiny vase.
   (a) dried
   (b) moulded
   (c) glazed
   (d) sucked

9. Place the crystal snail on the bottom <u>shelf</u>.
   (a) ledge
   (b) board
   (c) section
   (d) file

Circle the correct word in brackets.

10. I was (sandwich, sandwiched) between my pop and my nanna.

11. Dad's (neice, niece) and nephew arrived from England last night.

12. The (mountain, moutain) road is rough and highly dangerous.

## Grammar and Punctuation

13. Underline the **adjectives** in these sentences.

    It was a peaceful night. Millions of twinkling stars filled the dark sky. Suddenly, a shooting star flew across the shiny moon.

14. Punctuate and capitalise this sentence.

    im never going into the bears house again cried goldilocks

    ______________________________

    ______________________________

## Number and Algebra

1.

| + | 3 | 9 | 4 | 1 | 0 | 80 |
|---|---|---|---|---|---|---|
| 8 | | | | | | |

2.

| – | 9 | 13 | 11 | 15 | 17 | 88 |
|---|---|---|---|---|---|---|
| 8 | | | | | | |

3.

| ÷ | 56 | 32 | 16 | 8 | 24 | 88 |
|---|---|---|---|---|---|---|
| 8 | | | | | | |

4. Write the number for:
2000 + 500 + 80 + 2 = ☐

5. Complete:
481, 483, ☐, ☐, ☐

6. Complete the labels for this model.

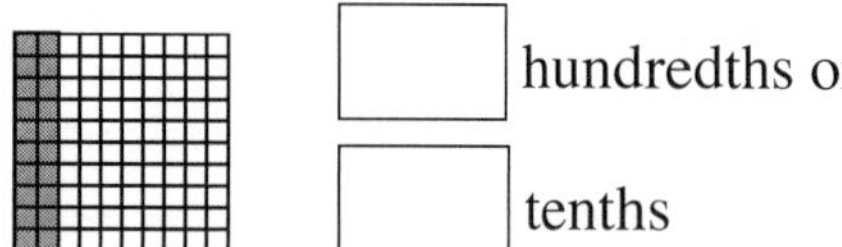

☐ hundredths or

☐ tenths

7. How much more do I need to make $200?

$50 $50 $50 ☐

8. Complete this label.

| Ones | • | Tenths | Hundredths |
|---|---|---|---|
| 0 | • | | |

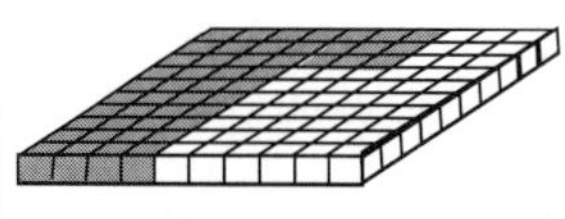

9. Circle the best estimate.
A pencil is two centimetres, fifty-six centimetres or ten centimetres long?

10. Wesley baked three trays of biscuits with 25 biscuits on each tray. How many biscuits altogether? ☐

## Measurement and Geometry

11. What time am I?
I am 12 minutes after midday. ☐ :

12. Draw a line segment that is 7.5 cm long.

☐

13. True or False? The top of a lunchbox is about one square metre in area. ☐

14. A mechanic poured three L bottles of motor oil into a large 20 L drum. How many more litres are needed to fill the drum? ☐

15. What is the boiling point of water? ☐

16. Is this shape rigid? ☐

17. Which solid shape am I?
I have one curved surface and no flat surfaces. I can roll easily.

☐

18. Which triangle has sharp angles only?

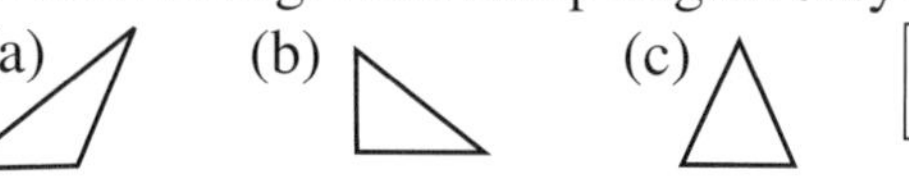


☐

19. Complete the picture.

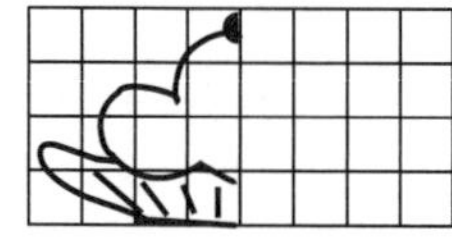

20. Describe the position of the letter X.

| X | Y | Z |
|---|---|---|
| T | U | L |
| K | G | B |

☐

## Statistics and Probability

21. The Girl Guides washed cars to raise money. On Monday 10 cars were washed, on Tuesday 20 cars and on Wednesday 15. Complete the picture graph to show this data.

## A Giant Leap for Mankind

Dreams do come true . . .

On 20 July 1969, a vision was finally achieved. Three American astronauts were sent on a moon mission aboard the Apollo 11. The first thing they discovered was that the moon's surface is covered in a grey dust which resembles powdered charcoal. The dust is thick and the footprints of Neil Armstrong (the first man) and Edwin Aldrin still sit on the surface today. That's because there is no wind or rain on the moon to erase them.

These two astronauts walked on the moon. The oxygen packs strapped to their backs gave them about four hours of life on the moon. Their main task was to collect rock and dirt samples to bring home to Earth. The 'Stars and Stripes' banner was planted. A TV camera positioned at the bottom of the spacecraft's ladder recorded this scene and those famous kangaroo hops.

Armstrong's first words were: "That's one small step for a man, but a giant leap for mankind."

The Eagle had made a perfect landing.

### Reading and Comprehension

**1.** Who walked on the moon first?
(a) the Russians (b) Michael Collins
(c) Neil Armstrong (d) Edwin Aldrin

**2.** How long did the Americans moonwalk for?
(a) 3 hours
(b) 2 hours
(c) 4 hours
(d) $4 \times 2 = 8$ hours

**3.** The 'Stars and Stripes' banner refers to
(a) the Russian flag.
(b) the TV cameras.
(c) the spacesuits.
(d) the American flag.

**4.** Why are the footprints still present today?

______________________________

**5.** Number these sentences in order (1–4).
(a) Two American astronauts walked on the moon.
(b) The TV cameras recorded the actions.
(c) They collected some rock samples.
(d) The Eagle landed.

### Spelling and Vocabulary

Rewrite the misspelt words.

**6.** Delia felt stranj on her first day at her new school. ______________

**7.** I grabbed a new sheat of paper and started a letter. ______________

Circle the word that has the nearest meaning to the underlined word.

**8.** The chairs in our new room were evenly <u>spaced</u>.
(a) cleaned (b) made
(c) stamped (d) arranged

**9.** My mum reckons Dad's a <u>sound</u> sleeper.
(a) snoring (b) good
(c) loud (d) deep

Circle the correct word in brackets.

**10.** Guards are (station, stationed) at Buckingham Palace.

**11.** Can you draw a (strait, straight) line which is broken?

**12.** My little sister always swims in the (shallow, shallowy) end.

### Grammar and Punctuation

**13.** Underline the **pronouns** in these sentences.

Those children did it. I don't like the way they tell lies. My teacher asked me for the truth.

**14.** Punctuate and capitalise this sentence.

in august our penpals from san francisco will be staying in sydney for a month

______________________________

______________________________

______________________________

# Mathematics



## Number and Algebra

1.

| + | 3 | 7 | 0 | 10 | 6 | 90 |
|---|---|---|---|---|---|---|
| 10 | | | | | | |

2.

| – | 10 | 15 | 20 | 11 | 14 | 110 |
|---|---|---|---|---|---|---|
| 10 | | | | | | |

3.

| × | 3 | 9 | 1 | 8 | 6 | 10 |
|---|---|---|---|---|---|---|
| 10 | | | | | | |

4. Which number is made up of five thousands, three hundreds and four ones? ☐

5. Complete this sequence. 1004, 1003, ☐, ☐, ☐

6. Colour part of this group to show $3\frac{1}{2}$. ♡ ♡ ♡ ♡ ♡ ♡

7. How many $20 notes have the same value as:

(a) $60? ☐ (b) $140? ☐

8. Complete the labels.

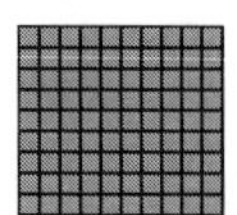 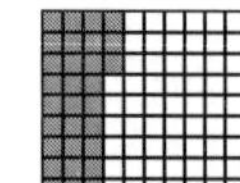

1 and ☐ hundredths

OR 1.☐

9. Round these numbers to the nearest hundred.

(a) 928 ☐ (b) 608 ☐

(c) 243 ☐

10. 8550 tickets. 5550 sold. How many tickets are not sold? ☐

## Measurement and Geometry

11. 120 minutes = ☐ hours

12. 305 cm = ☐ m ☐ cm

13. What is the area of the rectangle below?

☐

14. Yes or No?
Eva used more than a litre of shampoo on her hair in one wash. ☐

15. A thermometer measures

_ _ _ _ _ _ _ _ _ _ _ .

16. Draw an irregular hexagon. ☐

17. Here is the bed. Draw its view from the top. ☐

18. True or False? If the arms of each angle below are the same length, then the angles are the same size too.

☐

19. Write down a letter of the alphabet which has no axes of symmetry. ☐

20.

| | | | | |
|---|---|---|---|---|
| C | S | L | T | D |
| B | R | G | E | I |
| A | Q | F | H | P |
| | 1 | 2 | 3 | 4 |

Where is P? ☐

## Statistics and Probability

21.

| *Travel Method* | *No. of people* |
|---|---|
| Bus | 32 |
| Car | 40 |
| Walk | 28 |
| Train | 16 |

How many people took part in this survey? ☐

## Signpost Reading!

## Reading and Comprehension

1. Sign 1 means that you are not allowed to
   (a) brake. (b) turn right.
   (c) turn left. (d) turn back.

2. Which sign means that you need to be wary of pedestrians crossing the road?
   (a) signs 3 and 10
   (b) sign 10
   (c) sign 5
   (d) signs 5 and 10

3. Study sign 2. You park your car on Sunday at 12:30 pm. Are you allowed to do so?
   (a) yes
   (b) no, you need to stay there till 9:30 pm
   (c) no
   (d) only if you got there at 8:30 am

4. Which side of the road do we drive on in Australia? ____________________

5. Number these street names in alphabetical order (1–5).
   (a) Kangaroo
   (b) Emu
   (c) Koala
   (d) Platypus
   (e) Dingo

## Spelling and Vocabulary

Rewrite the misspelt words.

6. My favourite seazon is when the cherries appear. ____________________

7. I noticed that the engine room was completely filled with steem.

   ____________________

Circle the word that has the nearest meaning to the underlined word.

8. The man wanted to <u>shower</u> gifts on his wife.
   (a) surprise
   (b) hide
   (c) conceal
   (d) endow

9. When we shifted house, we <u>stored</u> our furniture.
   (a) bought (b) kept
   (c) exchanged (d) sold

Circle the correct word in brackets.

10. Are those roller blades (you'rs, yours)?

11. (Whose, Who's) the girl with the red hair?

12. Can you see (anythink, anything)?

## Grammar and Punctuation

13. Underline the **verbs** in these sentences.

    The children sat quietly beside the campfire listening to ghost stories. Now, it was Bill's turn to tell a tale.

14. Punctuate and capitalise this sentence.

    do you often help lea with her spelling words

    ____________________

    ____________________

## Number and Algebra

1.

| + | 2 | 6 | 10 | 9 | 7 | 94 |
|---|---|---|---|---|---|---|
| 2 | | | | | | |

2.

| – | 11 | 13 | 9 | 3 | 18 | 91 |
|---|---|---|---|---|---|---|
| 2 | | | | | | |

3.

| ÷ | 12 | 8 | 16 | 20 | 10 | 90 |
|---|---|---|---|---|---|---|
| 2 | | | | | | |

4. Fill in the table.

| | Th | H | T | U |
|---|---|---|---|---|
| 6809 = | | | | |

5. Complete this sequence: 981, 982, 983, ☐, ☐, ☐, ☐

6. Match the fractions.
(a) 62 hundredths (1) 0.84
(b) 12 hundredths (2) 0.62
(c) 84 hundredths (3) 0.12

7. Write the value of these notes.

$50 $10 $5 ☐

8. Write in decimal form:
(a) 3 and 19 hundredths ☐
(b) 1 and 23 hundredths ☐
(c) 2 and 56 hundredths ☐

9. True or False?
1423 is rounded off to 1500. ☐

10. 1200 students. 300 students are ill. How many students are not ill? ☐

## Measurement and Geometry

11. 75 minutes = 60 minutes + ☐ minutes

12. Round off to the nearest metre.
(a) 6.8 m ☐ (b) 9.1 m ☐

13. What is the area of this rectangle?

☐ triangles (△)

14. True or False?
A bottle of nailpolish holds about a litre of varnish. ☐

15. Average room temperature is about:
(a) 25°C (b) 70°C (c) 2°C

16. Complete the table.

| Shape | △ | □ | ○ |
|---|---|---|---|
| Name of shape | | | |
| Number of sides | | | |
| Axes of symmetry | | | |

17. Does this shape have any parallel sides?

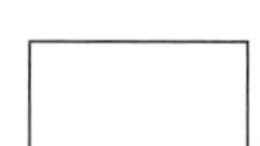

18. Shade in yellow the blunt angle.

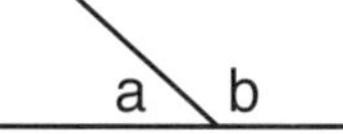


19. Draw a face mask which has no axes of symmetry. ☐

20.

| | | | | | | |
|---|---|---|---|---|---|---|
| B | ♣ | ➻ | --- | + | × | |
| A | ☆ | ❒ | ○ | ✓ | ? | – |
| | 1 | 2 | 3 | 4 | 5 | 6 |

What is in the position 3, B? ☐

## Statistics and Probability

21. Hair Colour in 4C

| | |
|---|---|
| Black | ♀♀♀♀ |
| Blonde | ♀♀ |
| Brown | ♀♀♀ |
| Red | ♀ |

♀ = 3 students

How many more students have black hair than red hair? ☐

## Jack Finds the Outback

"Is this the outback?" asked Jack.
"I reckon it is," said his dad.
"How do you know?" asked Jack. "I didn't see the black stump."
"Ah well," said Dad, "not many people get to see that."
Jack was sorry that he missed it.
That afternoon they drove off the Oodnadatta Track and bumped across scrub to Curdimurka. There they saw a long, low building. There were no windows, only holes in the walls. The wind whistled through the holes and when Dad and Jack went inside, they could see the desert through them.
"This is where the *Ghan* used to pull in," said Dad.
"What is the *Ghan*?" asked Jack.
"It was an old train that used to go through here to Alice Springs. Railway workers used to live here. But the *Ghan* doesn't come here any more, so no one lives at Curdimurka. It's deserted."
"Why doesn't the *Ghan* come here now?" asked Jack.
"Because they scrapped this line for a new one, miles away."
"Why?"
"Because they thought the old *Ghan* was too slow."
"It sounds pretty good to me," said Jack.
"Well mate," said Dad, "that's progress."
From *Jack finds the Outback* by Judith Womersley

## Reading and Comprehension

1. What was the *Ghan*?
   (a) a country town (b) Dad's last name
   (c) the black stump (d) an old train
2. The extract mentions the word *miles*. Today we use the word
   (a) electric train. (b) progress.
   (c) kilometres. (d) Ghanna.
3. The long, low building was
   (a) a railway worker's cottage.
   (b) a shearing shed. (c) a train station.
   (d) an outback homestead.
4. Name three towns mentioned in the passage.

   ______________________________

   ______________________________

5. Number these sentences in order (1–4).
   (a) Dad said that it was progress.
   (b) They saw a long, low building.
   (c) The *Ghan* was an old train.
   (d) It went through here to Alice Springs.

## Spelling and Vocabulary

Rewrite the misspelt words.

6. I'm always reminded about tucking in my school shert.

   ______________________________

7. My aunty and unkel have returned to the cattle station.

   ______________________________

Circle the word that has the nearest meaning to the underlined word.

8. Mary <u>soiled</u> her clothes at preschool.
   (a) sold (b) dirtied
   (c) sewed (d) dried
9. "<u>Lead</u> the way to your house", said the policeman.
   (a) lose (b) show
   (c) lavish (d) follow

Circle the correct word in brackets.

10. I wonder what's in (store, stall) for us at school today?
11. The helium (baloon, balloon) touched the hot light bulb.
12. Kangaroos and emus are both Australian (aminals, animals).

## Grammar and Punctuation

13. Underline the **adverbs** in these sentences.

    Dad drove carefully to church. Even though he wearily walked to his seat, he still managed to sing well.
14. Punctuate and capitalise this sentence.

    open the door please

    ______________________________

## Number and Algebra

1.

| + | 6 | 9 | 3 | 2 | 8 | 48 |
|---|---|---|---|---|---|---|
| 4 | | | | | | |

2.

| – | 8 | 11 | 14 | 7 | 6 | 43 |
|---|---|---|---|---|---|---|
| 4 | | | | | | |

3.

| × | 3 | 9 | 7 | 1 | 4 | 15 |
|---|---|---|---|---|---|---|
| 4 | | | | | | |

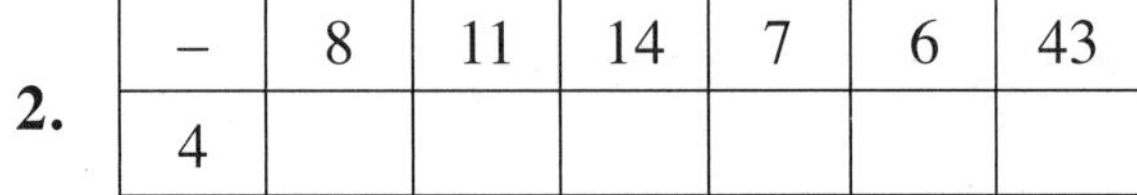

4. Write the number shown by the blocks.

5. Write all the odd numbers between ninety and one hundred.

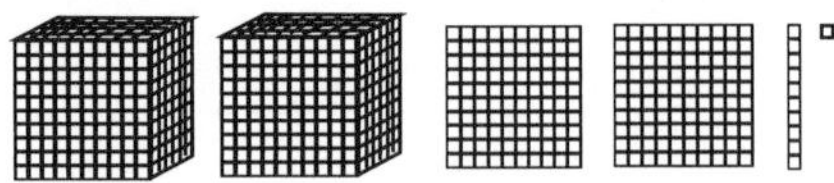

6. Study this box. Complete the labels.

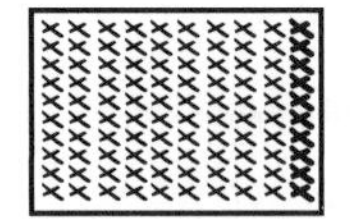

☐ out of 100

or 0.☐

7. How much more do I need to make $200? $100 ☐

8. Complete the labels.

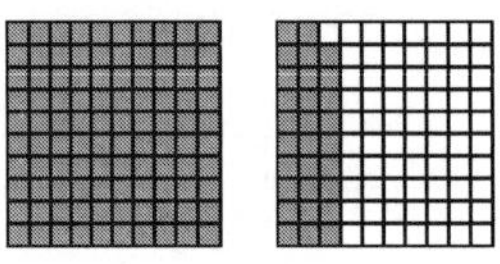

☐ and ☐ hundredths OR 1.☐

9. Circle the numbers that round off to 500.
453, 589, 501, 487, 469

10. Arnold bought 15 T-shirts that cost three dollars each. How much did he pay for the T-shirts?

## Measurement and Geometry

11. If Sunday is the first day of the week, what is the third day of the week?

12. Write these as m and cm.
(a) 170 cm
(b) 310 cm

13. Area = ☐ squares

14. Give the total number of litres.

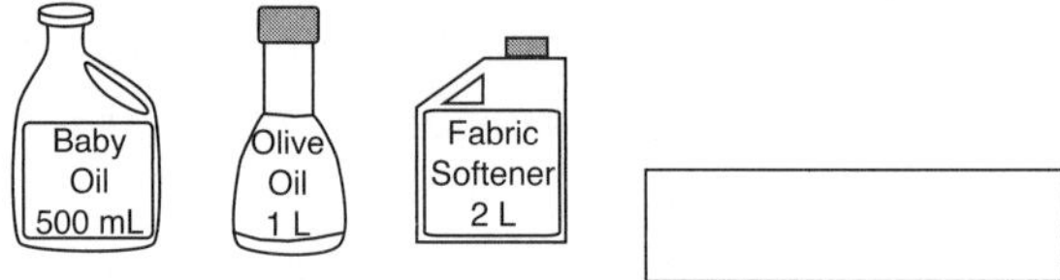


15. Mark 35° on this thermometer.

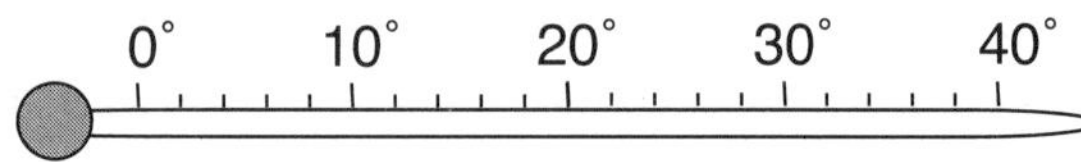


16. Draw an irregular octagon.

17. This is a t_ _ _ _ _ _ _ _ _ _ pyramid.

18. This angle is an _ _ _ _ _ angle because it is less than a right angle.

19. Draw a mirror image of this letter.

20.

| clips | rubbers | pencils |
|---|---|---|
| pens | tapes | staples |
| rulers | paper | pins |

What is kept second from left, bottom row?

## Statistics and Probability

21.

| Name | No. of Laps |
|---|---|
| Eve | ~~||||~~ ~~||||~~ |
| Ivy | ~~||||~~ ~~||||~~ \|\| |
| Jan | \|\|\|\| |
| Ben | ~~||||~~ \| |
| Elvis | ~~||||~~ ~~||||~~ ~~||||~~ \|\|\|\| |

Who swam the most laps at the Swimathon?

## Where's My Ticket?

She felt herself going red. Her hands began to feel sweaty and she trembled all over her whole body. She suddenly felt helpless.

*Where is it?* Penny thought. *Where can it be? I hope I haven't lost it! What will I do?*

Penny put all her things back into her schoolbag. She was very worried. *How will I get home?* she thought.

Just then, the train pulled into the station. Penny didn't know what to do. *Should I get on the train?* she wondered. *Or should I wait for the 4:05? Will I ring Mum at work? No, I can't—I spent all my money at the tuckshop.*

*Uncle David works close by; will I go and see him? No—he's interstate this week.*

*Oh, what am I going to do?*

Trembling, Penny sat on her schoolbag. She felt sick with worry.

*It's no use waiting for the next train*, she thought. *I still won't have a ticket. So how will I get home? Can I walk? No—it would take hours and Mum would get worried.*

Penny looked about to see if she could find a friend. There was no one she knew. Her friend Ann Bryson had not been at school today. Penny saw some of the other kids from her school, but she didn't know them and was too shy to ask them for help.

From *Where's My Ticket?* by B Reinholdt & H Andersen

### Reading and Comprehension

1. What was Penny searching for?
   (a) the train (b) her friend
   (c) her schoolbag (d) her ticket

2. What time was it when Penny arrived at the station?
   (a) 4:05 (b) before 4 o'clock
   (c) after 4 o'clock (d) before 3 pm

3. Which word sums up how Penny was feeling that afternoon?
   (a) lost (b) tired
   (c) shy (d) panicky

4. Which word in the passage means 'without help'? ____________________

5. Number these sentences in order (1–4).
   (a) Where is my ticket?
   (b) There was no one she knew.
   (c) Uncle David is interstate this week.
   (d) She went red.

### Spelling and Vocabulary

Rewrite the misspelt words.

6. Last Saturday, we had roast lamp, vegetables and bread 'n 'butter pudding for lunch.

   ____________________

7. The girl was being rood to me so I ignored her.

   ____________________

Circle the word that has the nearest meaning to the underlined word.

8. I'd like a <u>share</u> of the strawberry pavlova.
   (a) fifth (b) portion
   (c) cut (d) half

9. Rebecca is without a doubt a <u>sure</u> friend.
   (a) social (b) new
   (c) certain (d) reliable

Circle the correct word in brackets.

10. Three thirds is equal to one (hole, whole).

11. Why has this little (follow, fellow) been writing on the chair?

12. In walked the dentist, so happy and (bright, brite).

### Grammar and Punctuation

13. Underline the **verbs** in these sentences.

    Mum was waiting for me at the bus stop. She was tapping her fingers and checking the time. I knew she was angry.

14. Punctuate and capitalise this sentence.

    reverend martin is the priest at the catholic church in manly west

    ____________________

    ____________________

# Mathematics TEST 2

## Number and Algebra

**1.** Follow this addition path.

**2.** Follow this subtraction path.

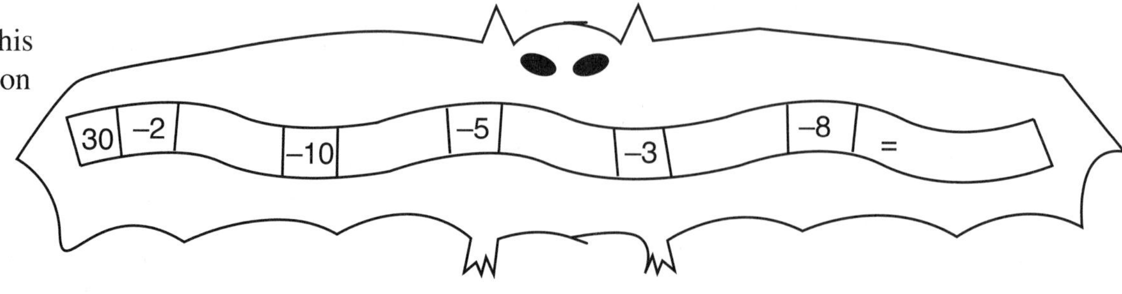


**3.** Complete these multiplication wheels. (a) (b) (c)

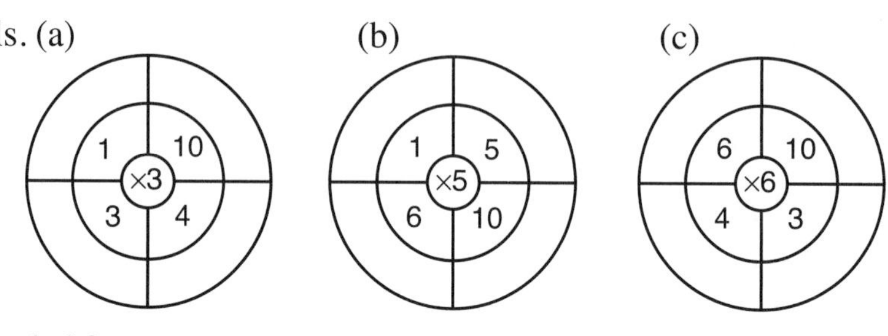


**4.** Write the following numbers in expanded form.

(a) 226 ______ (b) 109 ______

(c) 3862 ______ (d) 4603 ______

**5.** Jenny was counting in 5s. Go on in this series from 1270, 1275,

______, ______, ______, ______.

**6.** What fraction has been shaded?

______

**7.** Show $217 in the simplest way possible.
(Remember to use the least amount of notes and coins.)

______

**8.** Complete the label for each model.

(a)

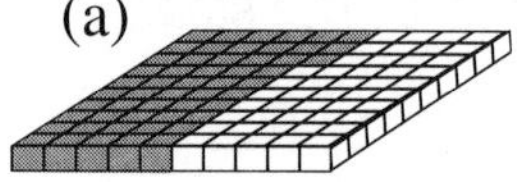

| Ones | • | Tenths | Hundredths |
|---|---|---|---|
| 0 | • | | |

(b)

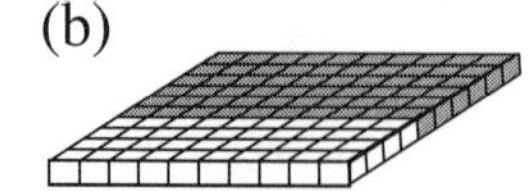

| Ones | • | Tenths | Hundredths |
|---|---|---|---|
| 0 | • | | |

**9.** Estimate how many circles make up this area.

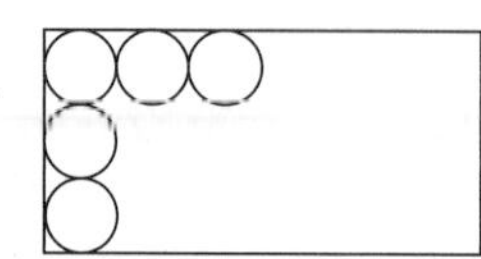

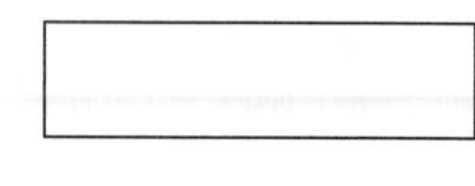

**10.** The trip to Nan's place took twenty minutes. The return trip took a quarter of an hour. Which trip took the longer time?

______

# Answers

## UNIT 1 page 8

### Maths

1. 6, 11, 3, 15, 9, 21
2. 1, 12, 15, 6, 7, 20
3. 24, 21, 18, 15, 12, 30
4. 68
5. 19, 21, 23, 25, 27
6. (a)

   (b) 
7. (a) $0.30 (b) $0.05
8. 0.20 (or 0.2)
9. 200
10. 6 × 5 = 30 yo-yos
11. 11:16, 16 past 11
12. (a) 12 kg (b) 20 kg
13. blackboard, kitchen floor
14. 3
15. very hot, hot, warm, cold, very cold
16. quadrilateral
17. 5
18. yes
19.
20. Mick
21. 10 seals

### English

1. c
2. d
3. d
4. $1.10
5. 1a, 2e, 3c, 4d, 5f, 6b
6. teacher
7. medicine
8. b
9. c
10. really
11. Whose
12. neatly
13. dinosaur, Brachiosaurus, metres, head, metres, ground
14. Rectangles and trapeziums are both quadrilaterals.

## UNIT 2 page 10

### Maths

1. 11, 16, 2, 10, 14, 20
2. 0, 9, 6, 17, 10, 19
3. 1, 5, 10, 7, 20, 21
4. 39
5. 52, 56, 60, 64, 68
6. 2 eighths
7. (a) $0.55
   (b) $0.10
   (c) $0.95
8. 0.50 or 0.5 (or half)
9. 600
10. 97–25 = 72 cows
11. (a) 3:20
    (b) 9:05
12. dog, brick
13. false
14. 9 l.
15. thermometer
16.
17. 8 corners
18. angle X
19. 2 axes of symmetry
20. 3rd shelf
21. 6 ice-creams

### English

1. c
2. c
3. c
4. tuckshop area
5. 1d, 2e, 3b, 4a, 5c
6. message
7. spread
8. d
9. a
10. heavy
11. missed
12. heal
13. led, decided, follow, came
14. 'How many times do I have to tell you to tidy your room?' bellowed Mum.

## UNIT 3 page 12

### Maths

1. 12, 8, 7, 3, 0, 50
2. 5, 12, 6, 8, 11, 50
3. 0, 0, 0, 0, 0, 0,
4. 164
5. 92, 94, 96, 98, 100
6. 1 fifth
7. (a) 60 cents
   (b) 40 cents
8. (a) 0.70
   (b) 0.30
   (c) 0.90
9. 500
10. 49 + 12 = 61 cards
11. (a) 10:58
    (b) 6:00
12. 8 kg
13. 8 squares
14. 12 cups
15. 50°C
16. c
17. 5 faces
18. parent/teacher check
19. 1 axis of symmetry
20. apple
21. 35 apples

### English

1. b
2. b
3. d
4. Northern Territory
5. 1f, 2a, 3d, 4b, 5c, 6e
6. wonderful
7. health
8. b
9. b
10. air
11. traffic
12. different
13. thick, tired, scratched, bitten
14. I'm not sure about David, Simon, Kevin or Michael.

# Answers

## UNIT 4 page 14

### Maths

1. 11, 15, 16, 18, 12, 20
2. 0, 12, 3, 7, 5, 18
3. 2, 4, 10, 6, 3, 11
4. 709
5. 59, 61, 63, 65, 67, 69, 71
6. 3 ninths coloured, 6 ninths not coloured
7. (a) 15c (b) 70c or $0.70
8. 
9. 400
10. 2 paths
11. (a) 9 past 6 (b) 38 past 10
12. 19 kg, 49 kg
13. 16
14. eggcup, teaspoon, glass
15. 91°C
16. 6 sides
17. 8 corners
18. turning
19. axes
20. top, left-hand corner
21. 2

### English

1. d
2. d
3. b
4. dedication, work attitude, approach to work, lesson creativity
5. 1b, 2c, 3d, 4a
6. Desert
7. family
8. c
9. a
10. reach
11. flower
12. stands
13. I, my, me, someone, themselves
14. 'Where did you put my soccer jersey?' asked the boy politely.

## UNIT 5 page 16

### Maths

1. 10, 14, 13, 12, 17, 20
2. 0, 6, 7, 10, 1, 9
3. 27, 81, 54, 18, 63, 90
4. 614
5. 984, 985, 986, 987, 988
6. 1 quarter coloured, 3 quarters not coloured
7. eighty cents
8. 
9. 189, 205
10. 35 children
11. answers will vary
12. 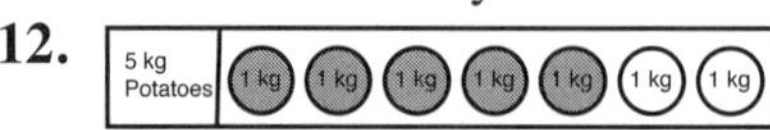

13. 1 $m^2$
14. half
15. 18°C
16. or similar
17. rectangle
18. straight
19. parent/teacher check
20. 9
21. 6 flowers

### English

1. d
2. d
3. b
4. a brief tale, legend or myth that has a moral
5. 1d, 2a, 3c, 4b
6. level
7. vase
8. b
9. b
10. cause
11. chief
12. charged
13. quickly, finally, slowly
14. We received an anonymous phone call on Thursday evening.

## UNIT 6 page 18

### Maths

1. 13, 15, 11, 17, 8, 26
2. 0, 1, 2, 3, 4, 14
3. 42, 36, 30, 24, 18, 66
4. 303
5. 647, 646, 645, 644, 643
6. 
7. $0.95
8. 75 hundredths (0.75), 49 hundredths (0.49), 68 hundredths (0.68)
9. 2900
10. +47, 56, +47, 103, 9, +10, +36, +37, +57, 66, 139, +73
11. minutes
12. $5
13. squared (metre)
14. 8 and a half litres
15. about 25°C
16. none
17. triangle
18. 2
19. A T
20. D
21. Teddy

### English

1. b
2. b
3. b
4. peaceful
5. 1d, 2c, 3b, 4a
6. holidays
7. through
8. d
9. a
10. care
11. carefully
12. course
13. over, under, to, of, before
14. Dr Julie Smithers is our local GP.

# Answers

## UNIT 7 page 20

### Maths

1. 15, 16, 10, 12, 18, 24
2. 1, 8, 10, 5, 12, 20
3. 2, 4, 1, 0, 5, 11
4. 218
5. 600, 500, 400, 300, 200
6. 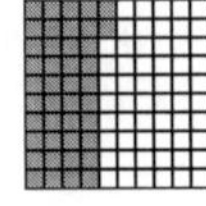
7. 50 cents
8. (a) 1.77 (b) 3.26
   (c) 1.50
9. false
10. $240
11. 30 days
12. 6 cm
13. kilo – gram
14. 

15. eighty-two degrees Celsius
16. b
17. 8 edges
18. 2
19. parent/teacher check
20. Portland and Melbourne
21. B

### English

1. b
2. b
3. c
4. a voice
5. 1c, 2a, 3d, 4b
6. cream
7. surprise
8. a
9. b
10. Merry
11. myself
12. Saw
13. Comets, pieces, rock, ice, Sun, path, Sun
14. Many of the prizes won by the athletes were still in the Principal's office.

## TEST  1 page 22

### Maths

1. 15, 18, 24, 26, 31
2. 20, 17, 13, 7
3. 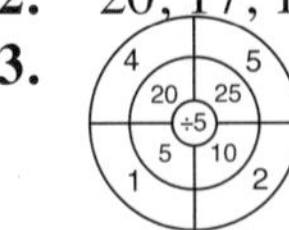

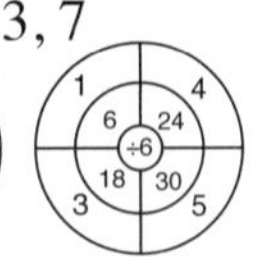

4. 4 5①8
5. 9645, 9646, 9647
6. 
7. $16
8. (a) 1.38 (b) 3.92
9. parent/teacher check
10. 200 m
11. 366
12. 30 kg
13. 26 squares
14. 25 L
15. 20 degrees Celsius
16. a
17. pentagonal prism
18. A
19. 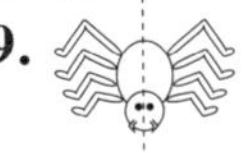
20. ✗ 3D, ☆ 5E, ❒4B, ❍ 6A
21. (a) Jan (b) 125 kg

### English

1. c
2. d
3. b
4. Cause of conservation
5. 1d, 2a, 3c, 4b
6. ambassadors, promoting, conservation
7. China, Panda, extinct, twenty-first, century.
8. living
9. reproducing
10. reserve
11. continue
12. 1b, 2d, 3a, 4e, 5c, 6f
13. panda, mammal, bones, animal, Pandas, humans, hands, thumbs
14. Fei Fei and Xiao Xiao were lent to Australia as a special Bicentennial gift.

## UNIT 8 page 26

### Maths

1. 16, 9, 18, 15, 11, 34
2. 1, 6, 9, 10, 0, 19
3. 9, 45, 81, 27, 90, 99
4. (a) 2433 (b) 7908
5. 1.94, 1.93, 1.92
6. 1 and 10 hundredths
7. $0.75
8. (a)
   (b)
9. 10
10. 6 × 3.5 m = 21 m
11. 7:23; 23 past 7
12. 1 m 60 cm
13. answers will vary
14. parent/teacher check
15. warm
16. oval
17. base
18. parent/teacher check
19. 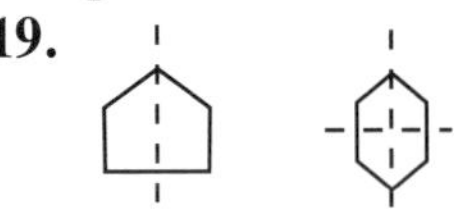
20. 
21. 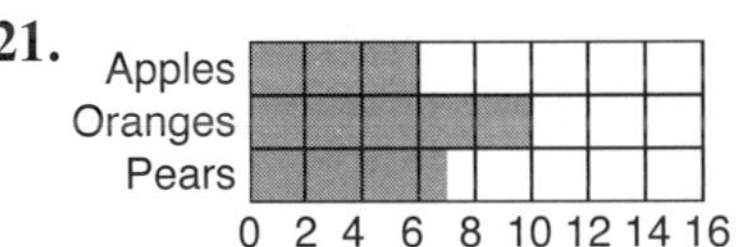


### English

1. b
2. d
3. d
4. less than half a kg
5. 1a, 2d, 3b, 4c
6. examine
7. visitor
8. a
9. d
10. accept
11. You'll
12. wrote
13. hill, cottage, scene, smoke, chimney
14. The little children were sent outside to play with the hose.

# Answers

## UNIT 9 page 28

### Maths

1. 11, 14, 15, 8, 13, 31
2. 5, 10, 0, 2, 4, 29
3. 1, 10, 4, 8, 5, 20
4. (a) 7
   (b) 60
   (c) 3000
5. 1.80, 1.81, 1.82
6. 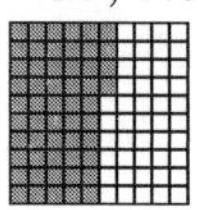
7. $0.75
8. false
9. false
10. 15
11. (a) 10:53
    (b) 5:59
12. (a) 125 cm
    (b) 340 cm
13. top of a matchbox
14. 20 L
15. a
16. regular
17. edge
18. d
19. parent/teacher check
20. parent/teacher check
21. 80 books

### English

1. c
2. a
3. b
4. interior, exterior
5. 1f, 2a, 3b, 4e, 5d, 6c
6. stove
7. sweep
8. b
9. d
10. wood
11. saw
12. male
13. on, near
14. Tim, the German Shepherd, waited for his master near the old, rusty gate.

## UNIT 10 page 30

### Maths

1. 8, 9, 10, 11, 12, 24
2. 2, 3, 8, 9, 1, 20
3. 14, 35, 7, 49, 63, 147
4. 2 145
5. 7600, 7500, 7400
6. parent/teacher check
7. 3 × 25c = 75c
8. (a) 1.37 (b) 2.20
9. false
10. 123, 110, 97, 84
11. (a) 48 past 9 (b) 30 past 5
12. (a) 1 m 70 cm
    (b) 4 m 58 cm
13. the corridor floor
14. 10 bottles
15. 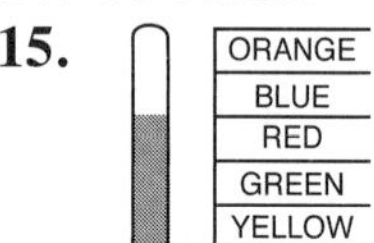

16. 4
17.
18. c
19. 1 axis of symmetry
20. red
21. 114 calls

### English

1. b
2. c
3. b
4. A legend is a story from earlier times.
5. 1c, 2d, 3a, 4b
6. speak
7. spoon
8. d
9. c
10. speech
11. spare
12. fifth
13. hen, box, egg, Mr Brown, pocket
14. I went to the Brisbane Library to borrow 'Quest Against Time' but someone had already taken it out.

## UNIT 11 page 32

### Maths

1. 12, 13, 14, 15, 16, 32
2. 10, 9, 8, 7, 6, 21
3. 60, 54, 48, 42, 36, 120
4. 4000 + 700 + 2
5. 6000, 5000, 4000
6. 7 tenths 2 hundredths
7. 6 
8. 0.14
9. twenty-six
10. 7 triangles
11. (a) 365 days (b) 366 days
12. (a) 1.25 m (b) 9.12 m
13. answers will vary
14. 120 L
15. 0°C
16. b
17. circle
18.
19. 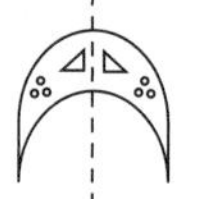
20. OOOOOOOOOOOO
    OOOOOOOOOOOO
    OOOOOOOOOOOO
21. 100 balloons

### English

1. d
2. a
3. d
4. Rigby and Lucy Lexine
5. 1c, 2d, 3e, 4a, 5b
6. serve
7. stir
8. b
9. a
10. sandwiched
11. niece
12. mountain
13. peaceful, twinkling, dark, shooting, shiny
14. "I'm never going into the bears' house again," cried Goldilocks.

# Answers

## UNIT 12 page 34

### Maths

1. 11, 17, 12, 9, 8, 88
2. 1, 5, 3, 7, 9, 80
3. 7, 4, 2, 1, 3, 11
4. 2582
5. 485, 487, 489
6. 20 hundredths or 2 tenths
7. $50
8. 0.49
9. ten centimetres long
10. 75 biscuits
11. 12:12
12. parent/teacher check
13. false
14. 17 L
15. 100˚C
16. no
17. sphere
18. triangle C
19. parent/teacher check
20. top, left-hand corner
21. 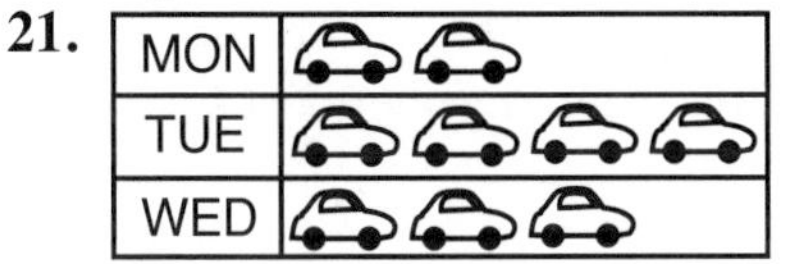


### English

1. c
2. c
3. d
4. because there is no wind or rain on the moon
5. 1d, 2a, 3c, 4b
6. strange
7. sheet
8. d
9. d
10. stationed
11. straight
12. shallow
13. if, I, they, my, me
14. In August, our penpals from San Francisco will be staying in Sydney for a month.

## UNIT 13 page 36

### Maths

1. 13, 17, 10, 20, 16, 100
2. 0, 5, 10, 1, 4, 100
3. 30, 90, 10, 80, 60, 100
4. 5304
5. 1002, 1001, 1000
6. 
7. (a) 3 (b) 7
8. 1 and 33 hundredths or 1.33
9. (a) 900 (b) 600 (c) 200
10. 3000 tickets
11. 2 hours
12. 3 m 5 cm
13. 6 squares
14. no
15. temperature
16. parent/teacher check
17. parent/teacher check
18. false
19. answers will vary
20. 4A
21. 116 people

### English

1. b
2. d
3. a
4. left
5. 1e, 2b, 3a, 4c, 5d
6. season
7. steam
8. d
9. b
10. yours
11. Who's
12. anything
13. sat, listening, was, tell
14. Do you often help Lea with her spelling words?

## UNIT 14 page 38

### Maths

1. 4, 8, 12, 11, 9, 96
2. 9, 11, 7, 1, 16, 89
3. 6, 4, 8, 10, 5, 45
4. (Th)6(H)8(T)0(O)9
5. 984, 985, 986, 987
6. 62 hundredths is 0.62; 12 hundredths is 0.12; 84 hundredths is 0.84
7. $65
8. (a) 3.19 (b) 1.23 (c) 2.56
9. false
10. 900 students
11. 15 minutes
12. (a) 7 m (b) 9 m
13. 10 triangles
14. false
15. a, 25˚C
16. 

| *Name* | Triangle | Square | Circle |
|---|---|---|---|
| *Sides* | 3 | 4 | 0 |
| *Axes of symmetry* | 3 | 4 | infinite |

(For equilateral triangle only)

17. yes (on base)
18. angle b
19. parent/teacher check
20. – – –
21. 9 students

### English

1. d
2. c
3. c
4. Oodnadatta, Curdimurka, Alice Springs
5. 1b, 2c, 3d, 4a
6. shirt
7. uncle
8. b
9. b
10. store
11. balloon
12. animals
13. carefully, wearily, well
14. Open the door, please!

# Answers

## UNIT 15 page 40

### Maths

1. 10, 13, 7, 6, 12, 52
2. 4, 7, 10, 3, 2, 39
3. 12, 36, 28, 4, 16, 60
4. 2211
5. 91, 93, 95, 97, 99
6. 10 out of 100 = 0.10
7. $100
8. 1 and 29 hundredths or 1.29
9. 453, 501, 487, 469
10. $45
11. Tuesday
12. (a) 1 m 70 cm
    (b) 3 m 10 cm
13. 12 squares
14. 3 and a half L
15. 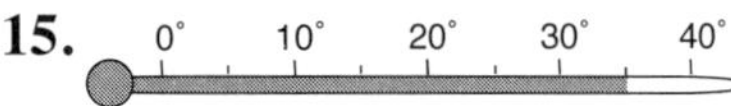

16. parent/teacher check
17. triangular pyramid
18. sharp angle
19. parent/teacher check
20. paper
21. Elvis

### English

1. d
2. b
3. d
4. helpless
5. 1d, 2a, 3c, 4b
6. lamb
7. rude
8. b
9. d
10. whole
11. fellow
12. bright
13. was waiting, was tapping, checking, knew, was angry
14. Reverend Martin is the priest at the Catholic Church in Manly West.

## TEST 2 page 42

### Maths

1. 22, 26, 36, 39, 47
2. 28, 18, 13, 10, 2
3. 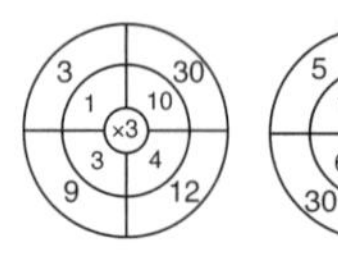

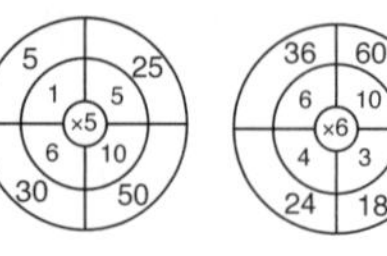
4. (a) 200 + 20 +6
   (b) 100 + 9
   (c) 3000 + 800 + 60 + 2
   (d) 4000 + 600 + 3
5. 1280, 1285, 1290, 1295
6. five sevenths
7. $100, $100, $10, $5, $2
8. (a) 0.53 (b) 0.60
9. 18
10. the trip to Nan's
11. 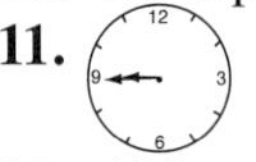 8:45
12. 425 grams
13. parent/teacher check
14. Travis's by 200 mL
15. 22°C
16. 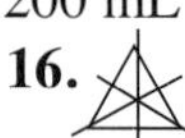
17. b
18. right angle
19. 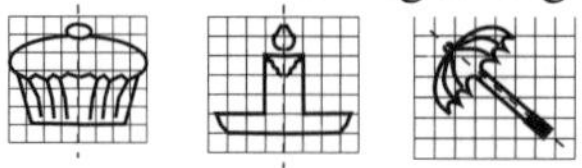 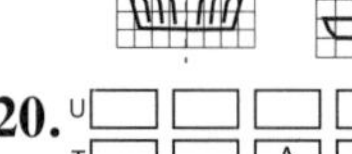 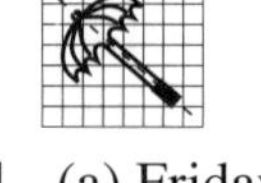
20. 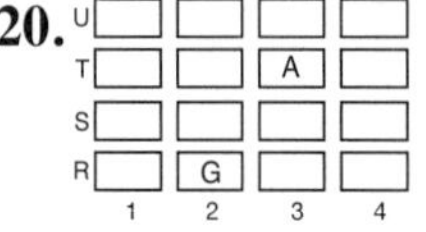

21. (a) Friday
    (b) 10
    (c) 56

### English

1. c
2. c
3. c
4. Previously, she had been tricked by Danny and Rose.
5. 1d, 2a, 3c, 4b
6. first, frog, teacher's, chair
7. helicopter, Miranda, walked, gate
8. a
9. d
10. know, thought
11. were
12. aren't
13. rode, laughing, went, pedalled, to get, hurtled
14. Miranda, Danny and Rose were looking forward to going to the circus on Saturday afternoon.

## UNIT 16 page 46

### Maths

1. 17, 13, 19, 10, 18, 100
2. 14, 13, 17, 18, 19, 10
3. 8, 14, 20, 2, 18, 90
4. 300
5. 25, 36, 49, 64
6. 5, 2
7. (a) $1.15 (b) $2.30
8. 72 hundredths is 0.72;
   43 hundredths is 0.43;
   62 hundredths is 0.62
9. 50
10. 9
11. (a) 4:07 (b) 10:50
12. parent/teacher check
13. 4 and a half squares
14. 1000 mL
15. (a) 62°C (b) 18°C
16. b and c
17. cylinder
18. 4
19. parent/teacher check
20. parent/teacher check
21. 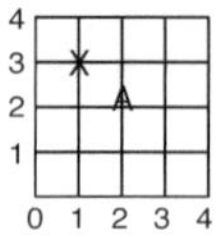 (grid: 0 1 2 3 4 / 1 2 3 4)

### English

1. b
2. a
3. b
4. (a) no (b) an hour
5. 1b, 2d, 3c, 4a
6. always
7. packet
8. c
9. b
10. What's
11. worst
12. wrote
13. marriage, Sunday, Church, Mrs Bettson, gown
14. The video 'Faint Whistle' cost me about twenty dollars to buy.

# Answers

## UNIT 17 page 48

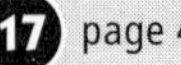

### Maths

1. 11, 5, 14, 12, 7, 101
2. 0, 6, 4, 11, 10, 90
3. 2, 0, 1, 5, 3, 20
4. 50
5. 68, 64, 60, 56
6. 4 and 2 left over
7. 35c
8. (a) 0.20 (b) 0.60 (c) 0.33
9. 70 minutes
10. (a) 20c, 5c
    (b) 10c, 10c, 5c
    (c) 5c, 5c, 5c, 5c, 5c
    (d) 10c, 5c, 5c, 5c
11. 4:34, 34 minutes past 4
12. 2 cm
13. 6 squares
14. (a) 356mL (b) 25 mL
15. 25˚C (warm), 16˚C (cool), 8˚C (very cold)
16. b and c
17. parent/teacher check
18. a-blunt, b-sharp
19. parent/teacher check
20. ✗ ✓
21. (a) $4 (b) $13

### English

1. c
2. d
3. a
4. Aboriginal
5. 1e, 2f, 3c, 4d, 5b, 6a
6. polite
7. pocket
8. c
9. a
10. pause
11. pencil
12. pray
13. sat, raced, did
14. There is a new pupil in our class who has been to Sydney, Perth and Adelaide.

## UNIT 18 page 50

### Maths

1. 15, 17, 27, 20, 25, 101
2. 14, 8, 15, 19, 2, 99
3. 0, 16, 40, 12, 20, 200
4. 4212
5. 3004, 4004, 5004, 6004, 7004
6. 5 and a half
7. 20c + 20c + 10c = 50c
8. 13 hundredths, 0.13
9. false
10. letter o
11. (a) 3 cm (b) 2 cm
12. (a) Wednesday
    (b) 5 Sundays
13. 6 squares
14. about 25 mL
15. 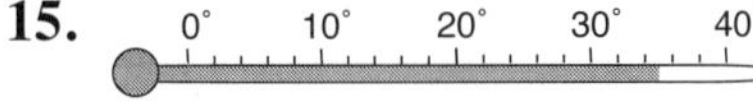

16. (a) circle (b) hexagon (c) oval
17. triangular prism
18. straight angle
19. none
20. Z
21. 11 o'clock

### English

1. b
2. a
3. d
4. Because the camera man was hit by the swing a few times.
5. 1c, 2d, 3b, 4a
6. knife
7. Music
8. d
9. a
10. taught
11. treated
12. return
13. blue, special, family
14. "What a hilarious tale!" cried Jack's grandad.

## UNIT 19 page 52

### Maths

1. 19, 11, 22, 18, 10, 101
2. 16, 23, 27, 19, 9, 101
3. 2, 0, 3, 1, 4, 10
4. 4215
5. 718, 618, 518
6. 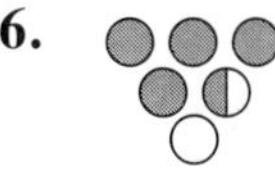
7. $1.10
8. parent/teacher check
9. false
10. 6561
11. 28 days clear, 29 days, leap year
12. (a) 65 g (b) 107 g
13. (a) $cm^2$ (b) $m^2$ (c) $m^2$
14. (a) mL (b) mL (c) mL
15. 0˚C
16. 8 equal sides, 8 equal angles
17. square pyramid
18. 
19.
20. New South Wales (or Victoria or Tasmania)
21. 卌 卌 卌 卌 卌 卌 卌 卌 卌 卌 II

### English

1. a
2. b
3. c
4. Graham
5. 1d, 2c, 3a, 4b
6. nature
7. knife
8. d
9. d
10. quiet
11. kindness
12. meant
13. our, I, she, it, it, his
14. "You naughty girl!" shouted my mother as she picked up the flower petals.

# Answers

## UNIT 20 page 54

### Maths

**1.** 19, 13, 15, 21, 18, 72
**2.** 18, 24, 12, 9, 6, 120
**3.** 28, 32, 8, 16, 0, 48
**4.** (a) 5
(b) 1000
**5.** 1564, 1554, 1544
**6.**
**7.** (a) $1.75
(b) $1.35
**8.** (a) 42 hundredths
(b) 58 hundredths
**9.** 20 m
**10.** parent/teacher check
**11.** July
**12.** (a) 175 g (b) 500 g
(c) 10 kg
**13.** parent/teacher check
**14.** 745 mL
**15.** hot
**16.** rhombus
**17.** triangular pyramid
**18.** parent/teacher check
**19.**

**20.** X
**21.** (a) Jim
(b) Elmo

### English

**1.** a
**2.** b
**3.** c
**4.** Ted
**5.** 1e, 2b, 3d, 4f, 5a, 6c
**6.** number
**7.** narrow
**8.** b
**9.** a
**10.** being
**11.** also
**12.** amongst
**13.** it, I, I, them, my, I, they
**14.** Do you think Annie was allowed to keep the greyhound?

## UNIT 21 page 56

### Maths

**1.** 19, 28, 38, 48, 58, 108
**2.** 6, 16, 26, 36, 46, 98
**3.** 5, 6, 2, 3, 6, 11
**4.** 1000 + 900 + 70 + 5
**5.** 9007, 9006, 9005, 9004
**6.** $6\frac{1}{2}$
**7.** $3.30
**8.** 4 hundredths
**9.** yes
**10.** 71 kg + 35.5 kg = 106.5 kg
**11.** (a) 70 minutes
(b) 1 hour 4 minutes
**12.** 500 g
**13.** true
**14.** (a) mL (b) L (c) L
**15.** 80°C
**16.**

| *Shape* | Pentagon | Hexagon | Nonagon |
|---|---|---|---|
| *Number of Sides* | 5 | 6 | 9 |

**17.** rectangular prism
**18.** parent/teacher check
**19.**
**20.** 2A
**21.** (a) $2 (b) $1.50

### English

1. d
**2.** b
**3.** b
**4.** gold, red
**5.** 1a, 2c, 3d, 4b
**6.** Tonight
**7.** tired
**8.** c
**9.** b
**10.** gentle
**11.** further
**12.** steal
**13.** wearily, busily, slowly
**14.** Quite unaware of the danger, Nicholas, the three year old boy, walked towards the boat.

## UNIT 22 page 58

### Maths

**1.** 11, 21, 31, 41, 51, 101
**2.** 63, 53, 43, 33, 23, 99
**3.** 36, 72, 90, 27, 54, 99
**4.** 7094
**5.** 85, 80, 75
**6.** $1\frac{1}{2}$
**7.** 20
**8.** 0.92
**9.** $6
**10.** 58
**11.** (a) 5 minutes
(b) 15 minutes
(c) 51 minutes
**12.** (a) 3000 g (b) 4500 g
**13.** 8 $cm^2$
**14.** 625 mL
**15.** 4°C
**16.** e
**17.** triangular pyramid
**18.** sharp
**19.** no
**20.** 10 + 5 + 0, 9 + 6 + 0
**21.** 25 kg

### English

**1.** c
**2.** b
**3.** d
**4.** spilling glue, getting stuck in the roof, falling off the ladder
**5.** 1b, 2c, 3d, 4a
**6.** timber
**7.** true
**8.** d
**9.** d
**10.** track
**11.** Either
**12.** entering
**13.** opened, smiled, hugged, gave, come, said
**14.** 'Jingle Bell Rock' would have to be my favourite Christmas song.

# Answers

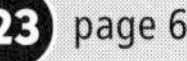

UNIT 23 page 60

## Maths

1. 15, 22, 14, 26, 9, 113
2. 6, 11, 4, 0, 8, 99
3. 2, 1, 7, 9, 10, 12
4. 700
5. 318, 418, 518, 618
6. 7 and a half
7. 20c each
8. 50 hundredths, 5 tenths
9. 2 m
10. 4 paths, parent/teacher check
11. (a) 60 seconds
    (b) 7 days
    (c) 24 hours
12. colour 5 weights
13. about 40 squares
14. mL
15. parent/teacher check
16. 2 pairs
17. 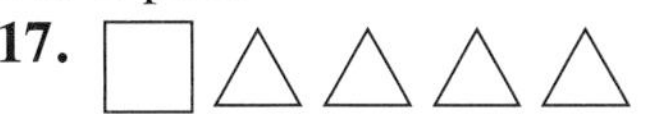
18. blunt
19. yes
20. parent/teacher check
21. (a) G (b) X

## English

1. c
2. b
3. c
4. (a) Sir Bill Kytes
   (b) Cyclone Brunella
5. 1c, 2d, 3a, 4b
6. ugly
7. upstairs
8. a
9. b
10. spill
11. fourth
12. forget
13. Jan, dress, shoes, Tuesday, Tylers
14. On my table is a box filled with paper, crayons, glue, tinsel and foam pieces.

TEST 3 page 62

## Maths

1.

| + | 1 | 2 | 3 | 4 | 5 |
|---|---|---|---|---|---|
| 6 | 7 | 8 | 9 | 10 | 11 |
| 7 | 8 | 9 | 10 | 11 | 12 |
| 8 | 9 | 10 | 11 | 12 | 13 |
| 9 | 10 | 11 | 12 | 13 | 14 |

2. 15, 13, 11, 9, 7, 5, 3
3. 1, 3, 6, 60, 60
4. 5 124
5. (a) 1680, 1580, 1480
   (b) 7000, 6000, 5000
6. (a) 7 (b) 4
   (c) 5 (d) 1
7. (a) 10 (b) 5
   (c) 3
8. (a) 0.32 (b) 0.64
   (c) 0.45 (d) 0.22
   (e) 0.61
9. (a) 200 (b) 200
   (c) 3400 (d) 100
   (e) 500
10. 6 m
11. (a) 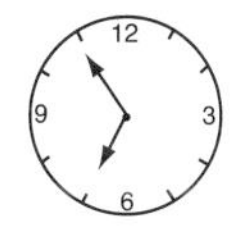

    (b) 

12. parent/teacher check
13. parent/teacher check
14. 6 $cm^3$
15. (a) 0° 10° 20° 30° 40°
    (b) 0° 10° 20° 30° 40°
    (c) 0° 10° 20° 30° 40°
16. 4
17. 6 faces, 8 vertices, 12 edges
18. b, a, c
19. (a) turn
    (b) flip
    (c) slide
    (d) turn
    (e) slide
20. (a) M (b) L
21. 23

TEST 3 page 64

## English

1. d
2. a
3. b
4. Literally refers to many cultures. In Australia it refers to our society being made up of people from many different countries and backgrounds.
5. 1b, 2c, 3d, 4a
6. sure, immigration, check, dictionary
7. miserable, bawling
8. b
9. c
10. migrants
11. cultures
12. past
13. down, in, towards, out
14. Help! I think I'm getting a migraine now!

# Answers

## UNIT 24 page 66

### Maths

1. 12, 16, 13, 15, 17, 76
2. 1, 6, 4, 11, 10, 58
3. 9, 45, 72, 81, 90, 135
4. 1101
5. thirty hundredths, thirty-five hundredths, forty hundredths
6. 4, 2
7. 2 ($20 and $5)
8. (a) 2.75 (b) 4.12
9. false
10. ●<br>● ●<br>● ● ●<br>● ● ● ●
11. 

12. true
13. 1 $cm^2$
14. 3 cubes
15. 90˚C, 70˚C, 85˚C
16. (a) 4 (b) 2 pairs
17. answers will vary
18. 
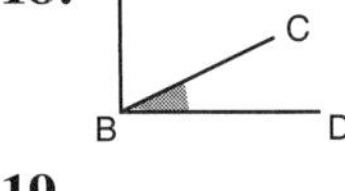

19. 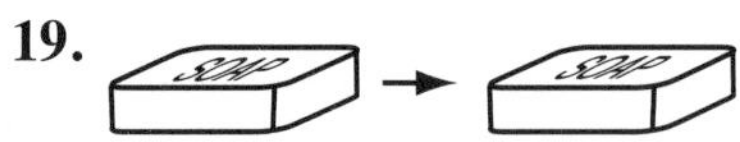

20. Go along Sunflower Rd, turn left into Rose St, turn right into Tulip Rd
21. 3

### English

1. b
2. c
3. c
4. tennis court, spa, walk-in robe, outdoor cooking area, air conditioner, alarm system, dishwasher, vacuumaid, sprinkler system
5. 1d, 2a, 3c, 4b
6. idea
7. electric
8. b
9. a
10. noisy
11. juicy
12. whether
13. man, business, January, money
14. The Qantas jumbo landed at half past eleven.

## UNIT 25 page 68

### Maths

1. 11, 7, 13, 16, 9, 80
2. 9, 11, 7, 14, 12, 68
3. 6, 1, 0, 4, 10, 25
4. 6302
5. 0.6, 0.5, 0.4
6. 3, 2
7. 7
8. 0.98 not coloured
9. false
10. 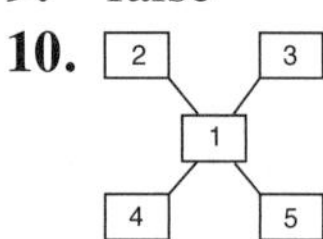

11. 3:16
12. false
13. parent/teacher check
14. 9 cubes
15. 13˚C
16. trapezium
17. square pyramid
18. right angles
19. parent/teacher check
20. ✔✔✔✔✔✔✔✔✔✔
21. 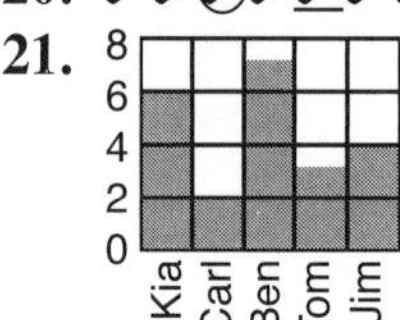


### English

1. b
2. c
3. d
4. 10 o'clock
5. 1c, 2d, 3a, 4b
6. cheered
7. Doesn't
8. b
9. c
10. paid
11. Aren't
12. cost
13. divided, checked, counting, tossed
14. My Auntie Beth wasn't sure whether to choose the orange, peach, lime or pink scarf.

## UNIT 26 page 70

### Maths

1. 17, 11, 15, 19, 13, 108
2. 10, 6, 1, 7, 2, 98
3. 100, 70, 60, 0, 10, 150
4. 3000
5. 0.88, 0.87, 0.86, 0.85
6. 1, 3
7. (a) thirty-two dollars<br>(b) eighty-seven dollars and fifteen cents
8. 3.33
9. true
10. ×, ÷
11. (a) 5:22 (b) 12:38
12. (a) 125 cm (b) 408 cm
13. 7 squares
14. 4 L
15. 4˚C
16. parallelogram
17. sphere
18. S
19. slide
20. 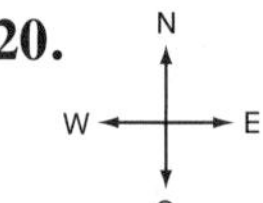

21. 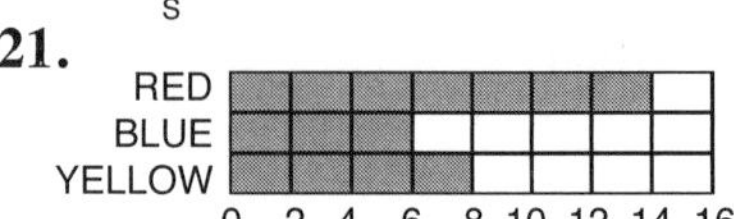


### English

1. c
2. a
3. c
4. The wings would melt and the feathers might become wet and heavy.
5. 1c, 2d, 3a, 4b
6. learnt
7. hurry
8. c
9. a
10. its
11. wonder
12. grassy
13. brass, wooden, striped, soft
14. The box that Timmy found was addressed to Mrs K. Logan, 34 Beans Rd, Ascot.

# Answers

## UNIT 27 page 72

### Maths

1. 20, 11, 18, 12, 14, 60
2. 9, 13, 6, 14, 8, 75
3. 10, 6, 2, 4, 3, 20
4. 1021
5. 2, 2.5, 3, 3.5
6. 8 and a half
7. (a) 3 people (b) 10 people
8. 1b, 2c, 3a
9. about 5 days
10. $107
11. past, second, old, face
12. 1.52 m
13. 4 $cm^2$
14. 800 mL
15. answers will vary
16. 1.6 cm,1.6 cm, 2.8 cm (2 sides are equal length)
17. yes
18. sharp
19. parent/teacher check
20. 
21. (a) $10 (b) Kris

### English

1. c
2. d
3. d
4. tidiest
5. 1b, 2f, 3d, 4e, 5c, 6a
6. knee
7. coast
8. a
9. d
10. chose
11. strike
12. spraying
13. merrily, everywhere, once
14. On 2nd November, we shall be competing in the Gold Coast Walkathon.

## UNIT 28 page 74

### Maths

1. 13, 12, 15, 20, 9, 112
2. 10, 6, 9, 3, 5, 99
3. 18, 48, 12, 54, 60, 90
4. 5119
5. 24, 30, 36, 42, 48
6. (a) $8\frac{1}{2}$ (b) $3\frac{1}{2}$
7. $5
8. parent/teacher check
9. $1
10. 42 eggs
11. (a) no (b) Saturday 5th, Sunday 6th
12. 46 kg
13.

| 5 cm | 3 cm | 15 $cm^2$ |
|---|---|---|
| 4 cm | 2 cm | 8 $cm^2$ |
| 3 cm | 3 cm | 9 $cm^2$ |

14. answers will vary
15. answers will vary
16. 2 strips across the middle
17. hexagonal prism
18. b
19. parent/teacher check
20. middle dot, 3.5 cm
21. column

### English

1. c
2. b
3. b
4. will not
5. 1d, 2a, 3c, 4b
6. won't
7. lawn
8. c
9. a
10. neatly
11. woman
12. anyone
13. he, his, his, I, my
14. Isn't it a brilliant spring morning!

## UNIT 29 page 76

### Maths

1. 11, 6, 10, 20, 14, 116
2. 10, 6, 12, 15, 17, 117
3. 10, 4, 5, 3, 7, 33
4. 50
5. 200, 250, 300, 350
6. parent/teacher check
7. $90
8. 1.03
9. cm
10. (a) 5 × 4 (b) 2 × 10 (c) 20 × 1
11. 12 months, 2 weeks, 52 weeks, 365 days
12. m
13.

| 2 m | 2 m | 4 $m^2$ |
|---|---|---|
| 4 m | 5 m | 20 $m^2$ |
| 3 m | 6 m | 18 $m^2$ |

14. 350 mL
15. 0° 25° 50° 75° 100°
16. 7 pieces
17. parent/teacher check
18. parent/teacher check
19. reflection
20.
21. picture

### English

1. b
2. c
3. c
4. pitcher
5. 1b, 2d, 3a, 4c
6. woollen
7. other
8. c
9. a
10. cousin
11. written
12. teach
13. in, on, out
14. "Don't forget to take your lunchbox," shouted Mum from the kitchen.

# Answers

## UNIT 30 page 78

### Maths

1. 15, 17, 10, 13, 19, 77
2. 10, 8, 0, 7, 4, 63
3. 70, 21, 35, 56, 14, 490
4. 6 thousands 8 hundreds 1 ten 2 ones
5. 7305, 7306, 7307
6. ▲▼▲▼▲▼▲▼▽▽
7. $20, $2, 10c, 5c
8. (a) 1.15 (b) 1.78
9. 15 minutes
10. 80c
11. hours
12. parent/teacher check
13. 25 $cm^2$
14. true
15. false
16. China
17. parent/teacher check
18. parent/teacher check
19. parent/teacher check
20. (a) Ken (b) 4,C
21. (a) 41 (b) odd

### English

1. d
2. d
3. c
4. began, started
5. 1d, 2c, 3b, 4a
6. cough
7. River
8. d
9. b
10. May
11. new, loudly
12. blew, candles
13. write, underline, see, cross, using, erase, check
14. I rang Ian Molloney to check on Tony's progress.

## TEST 4 page 80

### Maths

1. 22, 29, 37, 46
2. 20, 17, 9, 3, 0
3. 25, 25, 5, 5, 0
4. (a) 6 (b) 7 (c) 0 (d) 5 (e) 1
5. (a) 1.78 m, 1.79 m, 1.80 m
   (b) $3.00, $2.95, $2.90
6. (a) 6 and a half
   (b) 5 and a half
   (c) 7 and a half
   (d) 7 and a half
7. (a) $0.85 (b) $0.80 (c) $1.80
8. (a) 0.29 (b) 0.27
9. (a) 14 (b) 15 (c) 12 (d) 17
10. $5 \times 750$ mL = 3 750 mL $\times 5$ = 18 750 mL or 18.75 L
11. (a) 3:00 (b) 3:05
12. (a) 4m (b) 8 m
13. 50 $m^2$
14. 8 $m^3$
15. 0°, 40°, 80°
16. rhombus
17.

| Name | Faces | Vertices | Edges |
|---|---|---|---|
| Square Prism | 6 | 8 | 12 |
| Cube | 6 | 8 | 12 |
| Square Pyramid | 5 | 5 | 8 |

18. 180°
19. 1a, 2c, 3b
20. (a) vegemite
    (b) car
    (c) milk
21. (a) Friday
    (b) 5

## TEST 4 page 82

### English

1. b
2. b
3. d
4. about 60 birds
5. 1e, 2f, 3b, 4a, 5c, 6d
6. Vultures, locate
7. lays, eggs
8. d
9. b
10. know
11. were
12. close
13. (a) birds
    (b) crops
    (c) teeth
    (d) ostriches
14. When the baby swift is ready to hatch it begins to move inside the egg. The eggshell cracks and the pieces of shell fall off.

## Measurement and Geometry

**11.** Show quarter to nine in the morning on these two clocks.

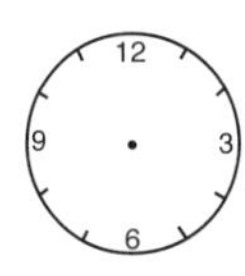


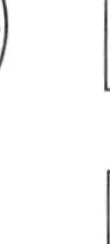

**12.** A loaf of bread weighs 850 g. Only half the loaf was used for lunch. How many grams were left?

**13.** Draw a square with a side of 2.5 cm.

**14.** Travis's custard recipe called for 2 and a half litres of milk. Mary's custard recipe called for 2 300 mL of milk. Which recipe calls for more milk? By how much more?

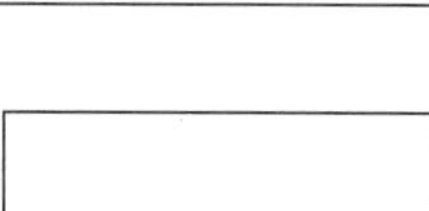

**15.** At 7 am the temperature was 12°C. By noon it rose by 12°C. By 3 pm it had fallen back 2°C. The temperature at three o'clock was:

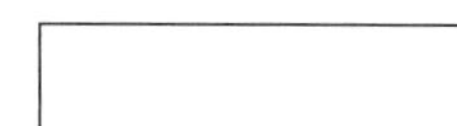

**16.** How many axes of symmetry does this figure have?

**17.**

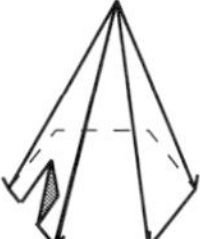

This tent best resembles a: (a) pentagonal prism (b) hexagonal prism (c) octagonal prism

**18.** Name this angle.

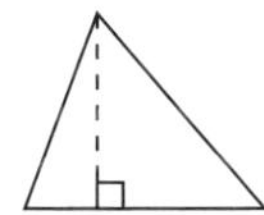

**19.** Complete each drawing along its axis of symmetry.

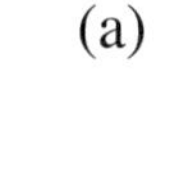

(a)

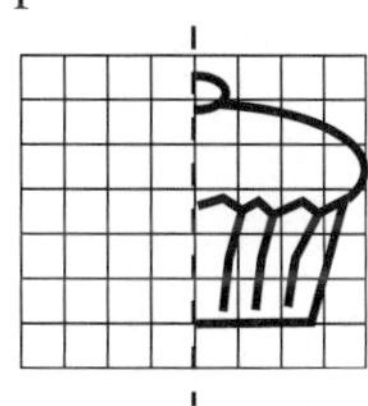

(b)

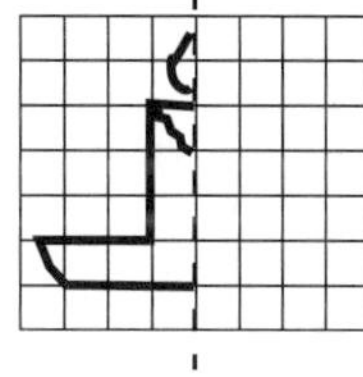

(c)

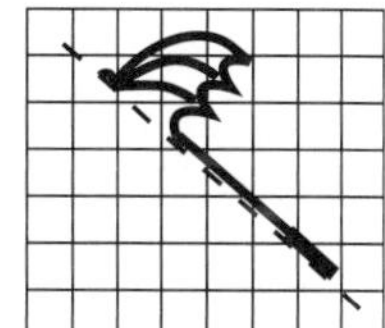

**20.** Write in:
- Amy is sitting in 3, T
- George is in 2, R

| | | | | |
|---|---|---|---|---|
| U | | | | |
| T | | | | |
| S | | | | |
| R | | | | |
| | 1 | 2 | 3 | 4 |

## Statistics and Probability

**21.**

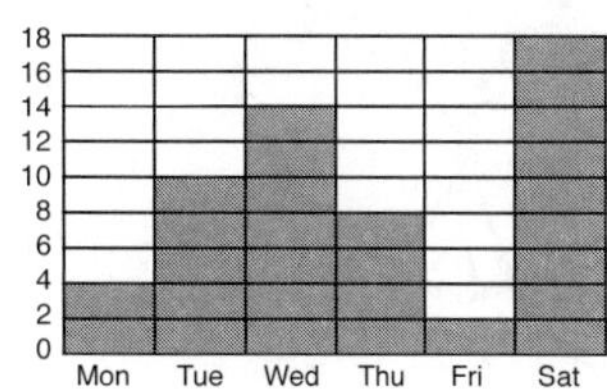


(a) On which day were the least appliances sold?

(b) How many more electrical appliances were sold on Wednesday than Monday?

(c) How many items were sold that week?

**Big April Fools!**

How can I trick Danny and Rose? thought Miranda. They've both tricked me. They've been practising every year, and they won't look. How can I trick them? I could point and say, "Look at the bird!" or "Look at the dog!" or "Look at the helicopter!" but they wouldn't look. They'd know I was trying to April Fool them.

Soon they neared the school. Miranda looked down a side street that ran to the park. She saw a row of circus vans painted red, yellow and blue. Then she remembered that they had seen posters all around the town for a week. The circus was due in town yesterday.

Miranda was about to say, "Look at the circus vans!" when suddenly she saw an elephant in the park beside the vans.

"Look at the elephant!" she shouted. "Look, Danny! Look, Rose! Down the side street."
"You won't catch me", shouted Danny. He rode on, looking straight ahead.
"I'm not an April Fool", said Rose. She rode beside Danny, her eyes fixed forward.

From *Big April Fools!* by Edel Wignell

## Reading and Comprehension

1. Who was playing the trick?
   (a) Danny
   (b) Rose
   (c) Miranda
   (d) the circus leader

2. Which verb does *rode* come from?
   (a) road
   (b) riding
   (c) ride
   (d) rowed

3. What stopped Miranda from telling them to look at the circus vans?
   (a) the posters
   (b) the helicopter
   (c) the elephant
   (d) Danny and his fixed eyes

4. Why was Miranda so keen on playing a trick on Danny and Rose?

   ______________________________

   ______________________________

5. Number these sentences in order (1–4).
   (a) The circus was due in town yesterday.
   (b) Rose rode beside Danny.
   (c) Danny rode on.
   (d) Miranda wanted to play a trick.

## Spelling and Vocabulary

Rewrite these sentences, correcting the misspelt words.

6. On the morning of April the fist, I put a frogg on my teacha's chare.

   ______________________________

   ______________________________

7. "Look at the helicopta," shouted Mirander as she walket towards the gait.

   ______________________________

   ______________________________

Which word has the same or nearly the same meaning as the underlined word?

8. Thomas played a <u>trick</u> on Tim by putting glue on his pencils.
   (a) prank
   (b) trip
   (c) tribute
   (d) riddle

9. They have been <u>practising</u> their trick for the last few days.
   (a) theorising
   (b) speculating
   (c) pulling
   (d) training

Circle the word in brackets which is the better fit in these sentences.

10. I (know, knew) how to trick them, she (though, thought).

11. They (was, were) sorry for the circus animals.

12. There (arnt, aren't) many circuses around these days.

## Grammar and Punctuation

13. Underline the **verbs** in these sentences.

    The children rode their bikes along the road, laughing as they went. They pedalled hard to get to the top of the hill and then, with a whoop of pleasure, hurtled down the other side.

14. Punctuate and capitalise this sentence.

    miranda danny and rose were looking forward to going to the circus on saturday afternoon

    ______________________________

    ______________________________

    ______________________________

    ______________________________

## Number and Algebra

**1.**

| + | 7 | 3 | 9 | 0 | 8 | 90 |
|---|---|---|---|---|---|---|
| 10 | | | | | | |

**2.**

| − | 6 | 7 | 3 | 2 | 1 | 10 |
|---|---|---|---|---|---|---|
| 20 | | | | | | |

**3.**

| × | 4 | 7 | 10 | 1 | 9 | 45 |
|---|---|---|---|---|---|---|
| 2 | | | | | | |

**4.** What is the value of the 3 in 9397?

**5.** Complete the number pattern: 1, 4, 9, 16,

**6.** How many groups of 3 pencils can be made from 17 pencils?

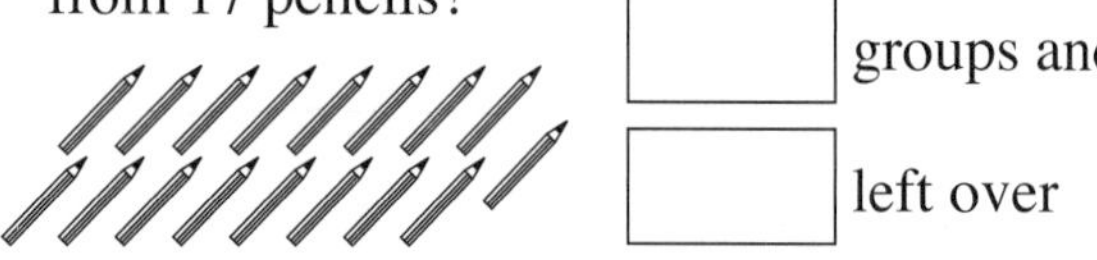

groups and

left over

**7.** Write the value for each set of coins.

(a) 

(b) 50c 50c 50c 20c 20c 20c 10c 10c

**8.** Match the fractions.

(a) 72 hundredths (1) 0.62
(b) 43 hundredths (2) 0.72
(c) 62 hundredths (3) 0.43

**9.** Circle the best answer.
The number of biscuits in a medium sized packet would be: 5, 50, 500

**10.** Six boys had an equal share of 54 marbles. How many did each boy receive?

## Measurement and Geometry

**11.** Write the time that is five minutes before:

(a) 4:12 (b) 10:55

**12.** Draw a line segment with a length of 6.5 cm.

**13.** What is the area of the coloured shape?

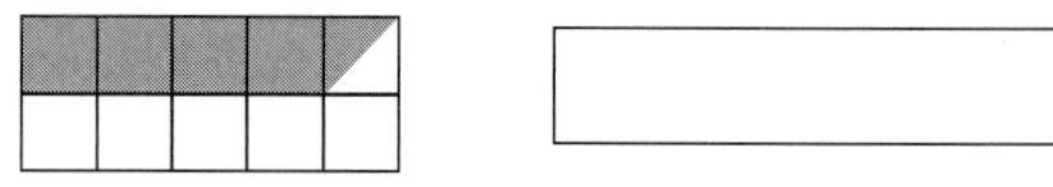

**14.** 1 L = mL

**15.** Write in shortened form:

(a) sixty-two degrees Celsius

(b) eighteen degrees Celsius

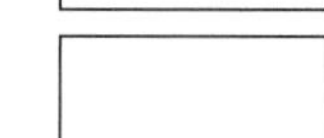

**16.** Circle the quadrilaterals.

(a) 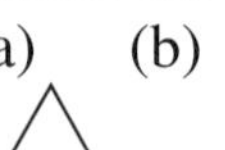 (b) 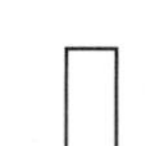 (c) 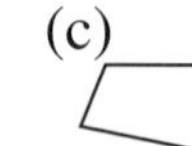 (d) 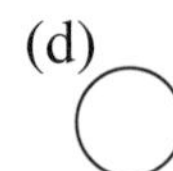

**17.** This tin of brown paint resembles which solid shape?

**18.** How many right angles does this letter 't' have?

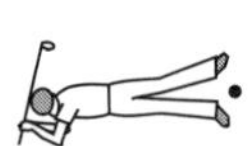

**19.** Turn this picture to the right. Use the golf ball as the pivot point.

**20.** Look down at your sharpener. Draw what you see.

## Statistics and Probability

**21.**

• Place an A on (2, 2)
• Place an X on (1, 3)

## Seen On TV!
### Monday

**Channel SGN**

| | |
|---|---|
| 6:00 | Tennis |
| 7:00 | Today |
| 9:00 | Here's Humphrey |
| 9:30 | Hunter |
| 10:30 | News |
| 11:00 | What's Cooking? |
| 11:30 | Entertainment Tonight |
| 12:00 | Midday with Kerri-Anne |
| 1:30 | Days of our Lives |
| 2:30 | The Young and the Restless |
| 3:30 | The Price is Right |
| 4:00 | Spellbinder |
| 4:30 | What's Up Doc? |
| 5:00 | Catch Phrase |

**Channel PST**

| | |
|---|---|
| 6:00 | Aerobics Oz Style |
| 6:30 | Cheez TV |
| 8:30 | Where you find the Ladybird |
| 9:00 | Good Morning Australia |
| 11:30 | News |
| 12:00 | Little House on the Prairie (series return) |
| 1:00 | Judge Judy |
| 1:30 | The Oprah Winfrey Show |
| 2:30 | Monday to Friday |
| 3:30 | The Brady Bunch |
| 4:00 | Totally Wild |
| 4:30 | Bold and Beautiful |
| 5:00 | News |
| 6:00 | M*A*S*H |

## Reading and Comprehension

**1.** What morning program, on channel SGN, is on at six o'clock?
(a) Aerobics Oz Style (b) Tennis
(c) M*A*S*H (d) News

**2.** If I turned on channel SGN at about three-thirty, which program would I watch?
(a) The Price is Right (b) Catch Phrase
(c) Gomer Pyle (d) The Brady Bunch

**3.** At what time does 'Totally Wild' finish?
(a) 4:00 (b) 4:30
(c) 6:00 (d) 5:15

**4.** (a) Is 'The Little House on the Prairie' series new? ______________

(b) How long does an episode last? ______________

**5.** Number these programs in the order they are shown (1–4).
(a) Catch Phrase (b) Here's Humphrey
(c) Days of our Lives (d) What's Cooking?

## Spelling and Vocabulary

Rewrite the misspelt words.

**6.** I orways enjoy making model aeroplanes.

______________________________

**7.** I went to the corner store and bought a two-kilogram paket of sugar.

______________________________

Circle the word that has the nearest meaning to the underlined word.

**8.** This <u>notice</u> will be pinned on the board.
(a) ignorance (b) sample
(c) announcement (d) number

**9.** It is <u>nearly</u> time for our Art lesson.
(a) ready (b) almost
(c) due (d) minutes

Circle the correct word in brackets.

**10.** (Whats, What's) the name of your German Shepherd?

**11.** This is the (worse, worst) bit of writing you've done.

**12.** Aunty Jo sat down and (written, wrote) a three-page letter to my mum.

## Grammar and Punctuation

**13.** Underline the **nouns** in these sentences.

The marriage will take place on Sunday in the Catholic Church. I'm going to become Mrs Bettson! My wedding gown is just about finished.

**14.** Punctuate and capitalise this sentence.

the video faint whistle cost me about twenty dollars to buy

______________________________

______________________________

## Number and Algebra

**1.**

| + | 6 | 0 | 9 | 7 | 2 | 96 |
|---|---|---|---|---|---|---|
| 5 | | | | | | |

**2.**

| − | 9 | 15 | 13 | 20 | 19 | 99 |
|---|---|---|---|---|---|---|
| 9 | | | | | | |

**3.**

| ÷ | 10 | 0 | 5 | 25 | 15 | 100 |
|---|---|---|---|---|---|---|
| 5 | | | | | | |

**4.** What is the value of the underlined digit in 46<u>5</u>9? ☐

**5.** Complete: 84, 80, 76, 72, ☐, ☐, ☐, ☐

**6.** How many groups of 4 oranges can be made from 18 oranges?

☐ groups and ☐ left over

**7.**

| | |
|---|---|
| Apples | 5c each |
| Oranges | 10c each |
| Mandarins | 15c each |

How much for seven apples? ☐

**8.** Complete the labels:

(a) 20 hundredths = 0. ☐

(b) 60 hundredths = 0. ☐

(c) 33 hundredths = 0. ☐

**9.** Circle the best choice.
Last night Jim watched TV for:
7 seconds, 7 hours, 70 minutes

**10.** 25 cents can be shown in 4 different ways. Draw them.

| | | | |
|---|---|---|---|
| | | | |

## Measurement and Geometry

**11.** Complete the labels for this time.

4 : ☐

☐ past

**12.** Measure the length of this paper clip.

☐

**13.** What is the area of the coloured shape? ☐

**14.** Use the short way to write:

(a) 356 millilitres ☐

(b) twenty-five millilitres ☐

**15.** Match each day with a suitable temperature.

(a) a warm day — (1) 16°C
(b) a cool day — (2) 8°C
(c) a very cold day — (3) 25°C

**16.** Circle the plane shapes with parallel sides.

(a) 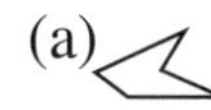 (b) (c) 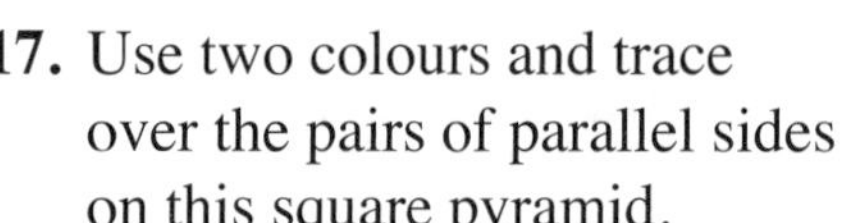 (d) 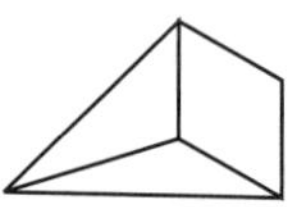

**17.** Use two colours and trace over the pairs of parallel sides on this square pyramid.

**18.** State whether these angles are blunt or sharp.

(a) 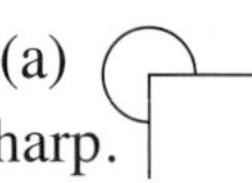 (b) 

**19.** Half of this shape is missing. Can you complete it?

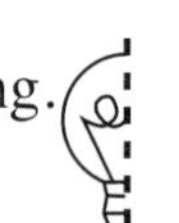

**20.** Draw an X in the top right-hand corner and put a tick in the middle of the rectangle.

## Statistics and Probability

**21.** CHARITY DONATION

Money given: $0, $1, $2, $3, $4
Lee, Tom, Senya, Ling, Kim

(a) How much money was given by Ling? ☐

(b) What's the total collection? ☐

## Choosing 'A' Baby's Name

BOYS

| | |
|---|---|
| Aaron | Egyptian—'high mountain' |
| Abdul | meaning 'servant', 'son' |
| Adam | 'man of red earth' |
| Adrian | 'Adria' is a city in Northern Italy |
| Ailan | French version of Alan |
| Alan | Gaelic—handsome, noble, rock |
| Albert | meaning 'illustrious' |
| Alec | shortened form of Alexander |
| Andre | French version of Andrew |
| Andrew | Greek—'manly' |
| Angelo | Greek—'angel', 'messenger' |
| Antoine | French form of Anthony |
| Armstrong | Anglo-Saxon—'strong arm' |

GIRLS

| | |
|---|---|
| Abbey | Hebrew—'father rejoices' |
| Ada | 'joyful', 'prosperous' |
| Adelaide | Old German—'noble kind' |
| Adina | Aboriginal—'good' |
| Adonia | Greek—'beautiful goddess of the resurrection' |
| Adriana | Italian—Adrian |
| Aileen | derivative of Helen |
| Alana | feminine form of Alan |
| Alberta | feminine form of Albert |
| Alicia | Swedish form of Alice |
| Alkira | Aboriginal—'sky' |
| Amy | Old French—'to love' |
| Angela | Greek—'angel' |
| April | month of the calendar year |

## Reading and Comprehension

**1.** What is the twelfth name on the boys' list?
(a) Andrew (b) Alistair
(c) Antoine (d) Ascot

**2.** Which girl's name is of Greek origin and means 'angel'?
(a) Angie (b) April
(c) Aura (d) Angela

**3.** What is the masculine form of Alberta?
(a) Albert (b) Bertha
(c) Berta (d) Alberthie

**4.** Of what origin is the name Alkira?

______________________________

**5.** Number these into alphabetical order (1–6).
(a) April (b) Amy
(c) Alana (d) Alicia
(e) Ada (f) Adina

## Spelling and Vocabulary

Rewrite the misspelt words.

**6.** Our school principal is always pollite.

______________________________

**7.** Ted found a twenty-cent coin in the pokket of his jeans. ______________

Circle the word that has the nearest meaning to the underlined word.

**8.** The <u>ladies</u> in the hall were playing Bingo.
(a) grandmothers (b) mothers
(c) females (d) sisters

**9.** Our visit to the zoo was <u>lovely</u>.
(a) delightful (b) good
(c) fun (d) alright

Circle the correct word in brackets.

**10.** I had to (paws, pause) so I could catch my breath.

**11.** Every morning I'm told to sharpen my (pensil, pencil).

**12.** I (prey, pray) it will rain soon.

## Grammar and Punctuation

**13.** Underline the **verbs** in these sentences.

The exhausted runner sat wearily on the grass. He raced his best time today. Fred did eight laps of the oval in thirty minutes!

**14.** Punctuate and capitalise this sentence.

there is a new pupil in our class who has been to sydney perth and adelaide

______________________________

______________________________

______________________________

## Number and Algebra

1.

| + | 7 | 9 | 19 | 12 | 17 | 93 |
|---|---|---|---|---|---|---|
| 8 | | | | | | |

2.

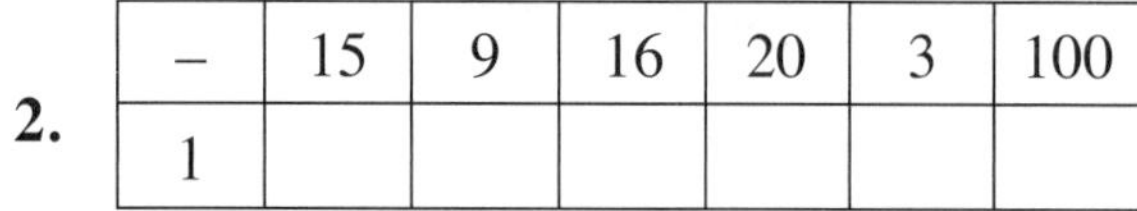

| – | 15 | 9 | 16 | 20 | 3 | 100 |
|---|---|---|---|---|---|---|
| 1 | | | | | | |

3.

| × | 0 | 4 | 10 | 3 | 5 | 50 |
|---|---|---|---|---|---|---|
| 4 | | | | | | |

4. Write the number shown on the abacus.

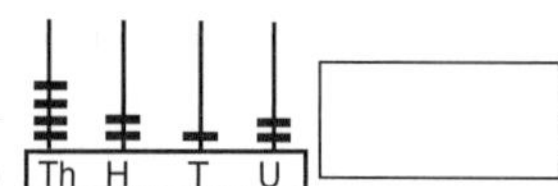


5. Complete this number sequence.

1004, 2004, ____, ____, 5004, ____, ____

6. Complete this label.

____ and a half

7. A pumpkin costs 50 cents. After buying one with a $1 coin, I was given three coins as change. What coins were they?

8. Complete the label for this model.

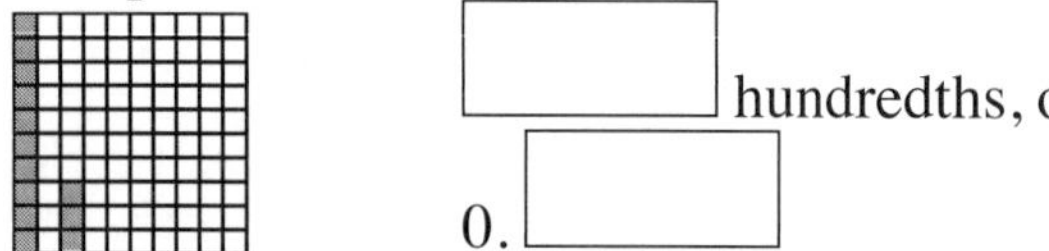

____ hundredths, or

0.____

9. True or False?
A two year old could carry a 20 kg piece of furniture.

10. Write down the fifteenth letter in the alphabet.

## Measurement and Geometry

11. Estimate, then measure the length of each bar.
(a) (b)

12.

| Sun | Mon | Tue | Wed | Thu | Fri | Sat |
|---|---|---|---|---|---|---|
| | | | | | | 1 |
| 2 | 3 | 4 | 5 | 6 | 7 | 8 |
| 9 | 10 | 11 | 12 | 13 | 14 | 15 |
| 16 | 17 | 18 | 19 | 20 | 21 | 22 |
| 23 | 24 | 25 | 25 | 27 | 28 | 29 |
| 30 | 31 | | | | | |

(a) On what day of the week is the twelfth?

(b) How many Sundays in March?

13. Find the area of this shape. ____ squares

14. Estimate the capacity of an eggcup in mL.

15. Colour the mercury to match the temperature.
35°C

0° 10° 20° 30° 40°

16. Write the name of each shape.
(a) (b) (c)

17. This net will form a:

18. Name this angle.

A __________ angle.

19. How many axes of symmetry does this shape have?

20. 

Which kitten has the string?

## Statistics and Probability

21. This line graph shows the temperature at each hour between 6 and 11 am.

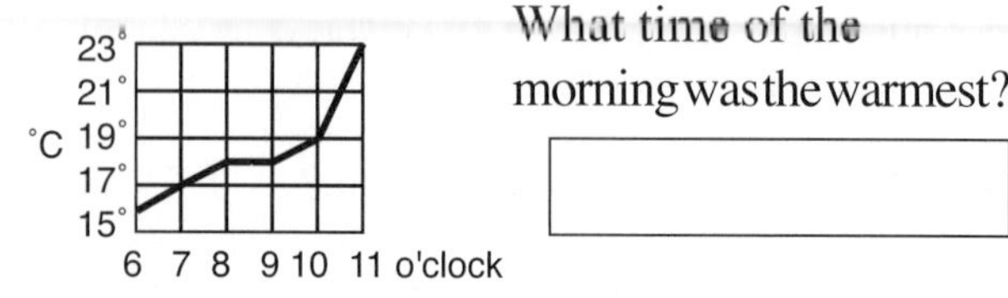


What time of the morning was the warmest?

## My Diary

1:20 Lunch was yummo today. Sammy gave us hot soup with little noodles, and roast lamb with big crunchy potatoes—I had three. I didn't eat any other vegetables. Who cares? Mum doesn't know. Then I had two lots of bananas-and-custard—my favourite. Sam also let me take the lamb bones for my dog Sandy tonight.

Enough of food. We only did two scenes this morning. They went OK. The sound technician had trouble because a dog a few houses away kept barking, and a man using a lawn mower decided to start up at just the wrong time. Richard must have called out "cut" a hundred times. He sent John, our second assistant, to try and shut them up (nicely, of course). It's funny how some people get aggro when we are trying to film something.

I didn't fluff any lines. Aren't I good? Poor Eric, the camera operator, had to film from a really awkward angle, behind the play equipment, and the swing kept hitting him on the head. I got the giggles, and we had to take a break so I could stop giggling, and Eric got a bandaid for his head.

Oh, time to be off again. Another wardrobe change and a check on my hair and make-up. Yukky!

From *My Diary* by Jenny Jarman-Walker

## Reading and Comprehension

1. What is the camera operator's name?
   (a) John (b) Eric
   (c) Sandy (d) Richard

2. How many types of vegetables did the author have for lunch?
   (a) 1 (b) 3
   (c) none (d) 2

3. Richard is probably the
   (a) writer. (b) sound technician.
   (c) actor. (d) director.

4. Why did they have to take a second break from filming?

   ______________________________

5. Number these sentences in order (1–4).
   (a) It's time for a make-up check.
   (b) I was careful not to fluff my lines.
   (c) We had a yummy lunch first.
   (d) We only did two scenes today.

## Spelling and Vocabulary

Rewrite the misspelt words.

6. Martin used the bread nife insted of the steak nife. ______________

7. 'The Sound of Musik' is my favourite video. ______________

Circle the word that has the nearest meaning to the underlined word.

8. My Uncle Jack has a <u>lean</u> face.
   (a) firm (b) lovely
   (c) loose (d) thin

9. Linda <u>chose</u> the blouse with the gold buttons.
   (a) selected
   (b) chewed
   (c) lost
   (d) checked

Circle the correct word in brackets.

10. Mr Thinly (taut, taught) me in Year Seven.

11. My dad (treating, treated) us all to a banana milkshake.

12. I had to (returned, return) the library book by Thursday afternoon.

## Grammar and Punctuation

13. Underline the **adjectives** in these sentences.

    After three weeks overseas, we were home again. Our blue suitcase was filled with special gifts for all our family members.

14. Punctuate and capitalise this sentence.

    what a hilarious tale cried jack's grandad

    ______________________________

    ______________________________

## Number and Algebra

1.

| + | 16 | 8 | 19 | 15 | 7 | 98 |
|---|---|---|---|---|---|---|
| 3 | | | | | | |

2.

| – | 18 | 25 | 29 | 21 | 11 | 103 |
|---|---|---|---|---|---|---|
| 2 | | | | | | |

3.

| ÷ | 12 | 0 | 18 | 6 | 24 | 60 |
|---|---|---|---|---|---|---|
| 6 | | | | | | |

4. Write the number shown by the blocks.

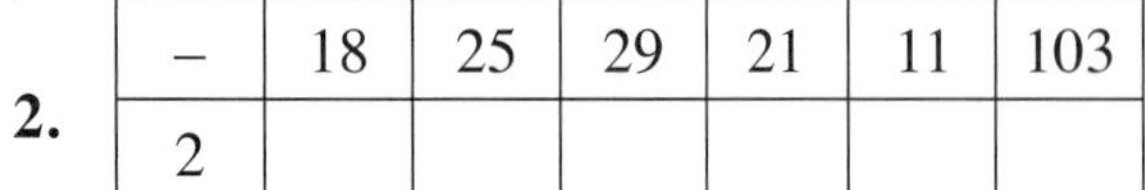

5. Complete this number pattern: 918, 818, ___, ___, ___, 418

6. Colour the part of this group to match the fraction. 4 and a half

7. Answer this money problem.
ruler $0.50
sharpener $0.60 Total cost

8. On this block shade the decimal fraction given. 0.43

9. True or False? One mug would fill a litre container.

10. Grab your calculator. Press 9 × four times and write down the 4-digit answer.

## Measurement and Geometry

11. February has ___ days clear and ___ days each ___ year.

12. Use the short form to write:
(a) sixty-five grams
(b) 107 grams

13. Choose the best unit of measure ($m^2$ or $cm^2$) to find the area of a:
(a) book cover (b) bedroom floor
(c) sports oval

14. Write L or mL next to each one.
(a) spoonful of cough syrup
(b) teaspoon of vinegar
(c) can of softdrink

15. Choose the best answer. Water freezes at:
60°C, 90°C, 0°C, 100°C

16. A regular octagon has ___ equal sides and ___ equal angles.

17. This net belongs to a:

18. Shade all the angles in this shape. The first one is done for you.

19. Slide this picture to the left.

20. Which state is south of Queensland?

## Statistics and Probability

21. Show 52 in tally marks.

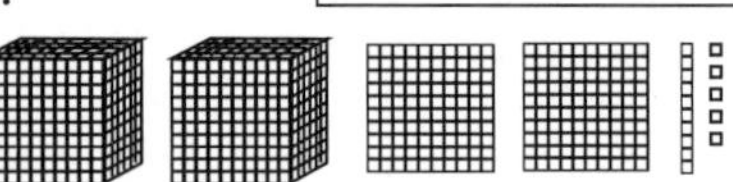
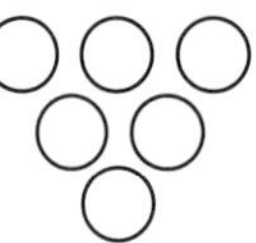
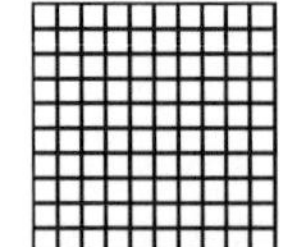
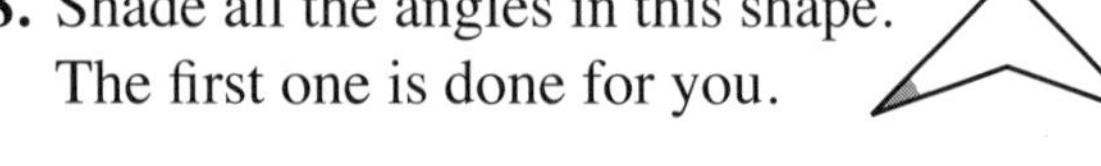

## A Night at Benny's

No one answered. The whole house was blacker than octopus ink. Along the hall we groped, into the loungeroom. Benny flicked a switch on the wall. No light.

"Felicity!" Benny called again. No reply. It was spooky, just like being in a haunted house at midnight on Halloween. I reached out and touched Benny. He screamed. "Don't do that!" he roared.

We stood together in the hall, listening. We heard nothing but the sound of our own panting breaths. Shadowy figures loomed up in the dark. My heart pounded faster than a prize-fighter's glove in a title fight.

"Ghosts!" I squealed, pointing at the advancing shadows.

"Help!" shrieked Benny.

We turned and ran. The ghosts grabbed us. For ghosts, they sure hit hard. They hit so hard we were knocked to the ground. They laughed as they clouted us: one-two, one-two.

"I told you I'd get even with you," panted Felicity. By the time Graham turned the electricity back on at the fusebox outside, Benny and I had recovered ... sort of. Felicity threatened to dob us in if we didn't go to bed, so we went.

From *A Night at Benny's* by Dianne Bates

## Reading and Comprehension

1. What is the best meaning for the word *grope*?
   (a) 'search uncertainly'
   (b) 'grab onto strongly'
   (c) 'gallop around'
   (d) 'be unable to see in the dark'

2. How many children were playing *ghosts* at night?
   (a) 1 (b) 2
   (c) 3 (d) 4

3. Where was the fusebox positioned?
   (a) in the hallway
   (b) in the bedroom
   (c) outside the house
   (d) on the ground near the octopus's inkbox

4. Who turned the electricity back on?

   ______________________________

5. Number these sentences in order (1–4).
   (a) The ghosts grabbed and hit us hard.
   (b) Felicity threatened to dob us in.
   (c) We heard nothing but panting breaths.
   (d) It was spooky.

## Spelling and Vocabulary

Rewrite the misspelt words.

6. My teacher wrote on my report that I have a pleasant naicha.

   ______________________________

7. Fiona dropped the fork and the nife onto the floor. ______________

Circle the word that has the nearest meaning to the underlined word.

8. The other day Alan wrote an <u>honest</u> letter to his friend.
   (a) long (b) hurried (c) good (d) sincere

9. The mother kangaroo was looking after her <u>babies</u>.
   (a) little (b) pups (c) family (d) young

Circle the correct word in brackets.

10. We spent a (quite, quiet) day bike riding through the botanical gardens.

11. Your (kind, kindness) in this matter will be greatly appreciated.

12. I told Mum that I only (meant, mean't) to be helpful.

## Grammar and Punctuation

13. Underline the **pronouns** in these sentences.

    The lost coin was somewhere between our feet. I thought she had found it first but then Max found it under his left shoe.

14. Punctuate and capitalise this sentence.

    you naughty girl shouted my mother as she picked up the flower petals

    ______________________________

    ______________________________

## Number and Algebra

**1.**

| + | 13 | 7 | 9 | 15 | 12 | 66 |
|---|---|---|---|---|---|---|
| 6 | | | | | | |

**2.**

| − | 21 | 27 | 15 | 12 | 9 | 123 |
|---|---|---|---|---|---|---|
| 3 | | | | | | |

**3.**

| × | 7 | 8 | 2 | 4 | 0 | 12 |
|---|---|---|---|---|---|---|
| 4 | | | | | | |

**4.** Write the place value of the bold digit.
(a) 930**5** (b) **1**607

**5.** Put in the missing numbers: 1594, 1584, 1574,

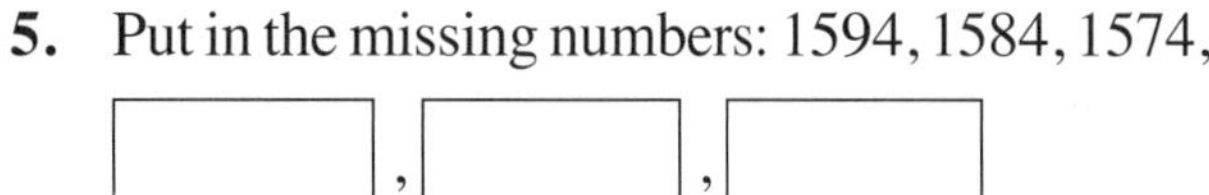

**6.** Draw 8 and a half stars.

**7.** Write down the total cost for each of these:
(a) $0.45, $1.30
(b) $0.55, $0.80

**8.** In this hundred square:

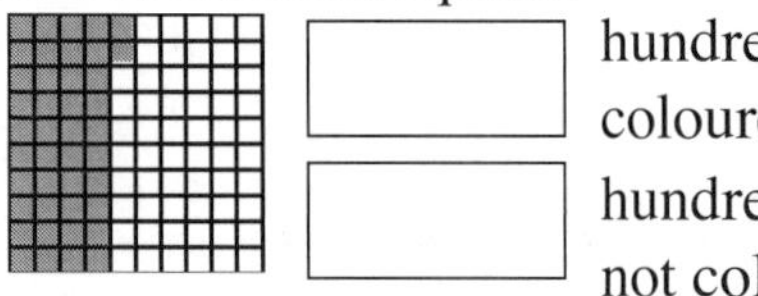

hundredths are coloured
hundredths are not coloured

**9.** Choose the best one.
A swimming pool is: 20 cm or 20 m long?

**10.** In this diagram, find a parallelogram and colour it blue.

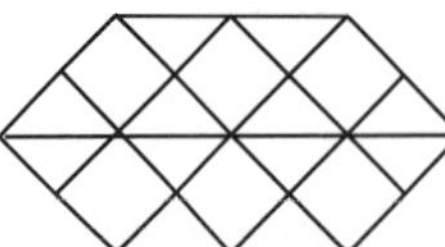

## Measurement and Geometry

**11.** What is the seventh month of the calendar year?

**12.** Which unit of measurement (g or kg) has been left off each package?

CHIPS 175
BUTTER 500
ONIONS 10

**13.** Draw a square with an area of 4 $cm^2$.

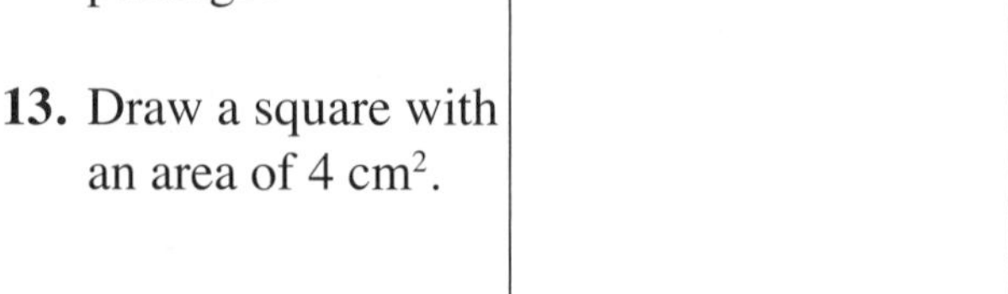

**14.** What is the total capacity of these containers?

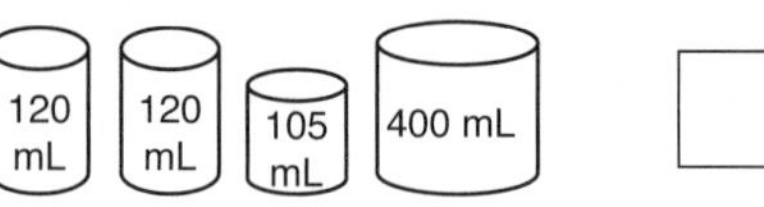


**15.** Fill in the missing letters.
25°C to 35°C is warm to _ _ _ weather.

**16.** What polygon am I? I have 4 sides which are equal. All my angles are not equal.

**17.** Write the name of this solid shape.

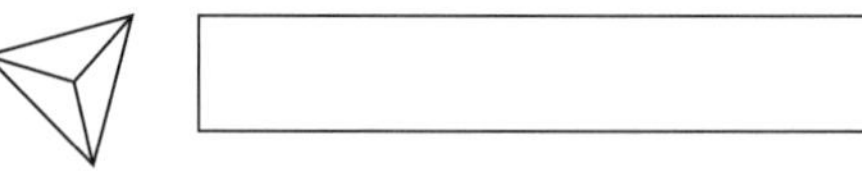

**18.** In box A draw a right angle. In box B draw a sharp angle.

| A | B |
|---|---|
| | |

**19.** Draw in the fold line on this piece of sporting equipment.

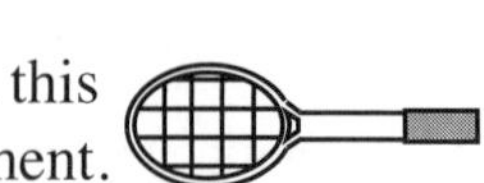

**20.**

| C | Δ | ÷ | ? |
|---|---|---|---|
| B | * | × | ∝ |
| A | ∞ | + | − |
| | 1 | 2 | 3 |

What is in position 2, B?

## Statistics and Probability

**21.**

CANDY
ELMO
JIM
BILL
TED
0 5 10 15 20 25 30 cm

(a) Which child has the longest foot?

(b) Who has the shortest foot?

## Jolly Jokes

Tim: Who delivers presents at the seashore?
Mark: Sandy Claus!

Rob: What did Santa say when one of his reindeer went missing?
Phil: No Comet!

Dena: What baseball position do all elves play?
Ted: Short stop!

Ling: Which Olympic Hockey team skates the fastest?
Magna: The Soviets because they're always Russian.

Gerry: Why did the snowman have a carrot nose?
Dennis: Tomatoes were out of season!

Lucy: What did Santa say when he bashed his toe?
Marion: Oh! Oh! Oh!

Jack: Did you hear about the ice-cube that tried to be a big shot by getting a sun tan?
Lee: No—what happened?
Jack: The big shot ended up a little drip!

Tony: What has pointed ears, makes toys for Santa and is four metres tall?
Carol: An elf on stilts!

## Reading and Comprehension

**1.** Who said the answer to the joke about the Comet?
(a) Phil (b) Jack
(c) Gerry (d) Jill

**2.** How many children ask the joke questions?
(a) 16 (b) 8 (c) 9 (d) 15

**3.** Whose joke needed another question before the punchline was given?
(a) Ling's (b) Tony's
(c) Jack's (d) Lee's

**4.** Who answered the joke about baseball?

______________________________

**5.** Number these words in alphabetical order (1–6).
(a) Santa (b) elf
(c) toys (d) merry
(e) Christmas (f) reindeer

## Spelling and Vocabulary

Rewrite the misspelt words.

**6.** Fiona was not sure of the numba after eighty-two. ____________

**7.** Dad warned Mum that the road would narroe ahead. ____________

Circle the word that has the nearest meaning to the underlined word.

**8.** Did you pack all the fishing <u>gear</u>?
(a) gum (b) equipment
(c) stuff (d) bait

**9.** Barney had to go and play for the other <u>team</u>.
(a) side (b) enemy
(c) sport (d) two

Circle the correct word in brackets.

**10.** While dinner was (been, being) prepared I did my Science project.

**11.** Tabatha (allso, also) bought a piece of cake for morning tea.

**12.** The bag of lollies was shared (amongst, among) three people.

## Grammar and Punctuation

**13.** Underline the **pronouns** in these sentences.

It was early when I set out. I grabbed those black shoes and tossed them into my backpack. I knew they were going to be on time.

**14.** Punctuate and capitalise this sentence.

do you think annie was allowed to keep the greyhound

______________________________

______________________________

## Number and Algebra

1.

| + | 15 | 24 | 34 | 44 | 54 | 104 |
|---|---|---|---|---|---|---|
| 4 | | | | | | |

2.

| – | 12 | 22 | 32 | 42 | 52 | 104 |
|---|---|---|---|---|---|---|
| 6 | | | | | | |

3.

| ÷ | 35 | 42 | 14 | 21 | 42 | 77 |
|---|---|---|---|---|---|---|
| 7 | | | | | | |

4. Write 1975 in expanded notation.

5. Write in the missing numbers: 9009, 9008,

6. Which is bigger, $4\frac{1}{2}$ or $6\frac{1}{2}$?

7. Answer this shopping problem.

stickers $1.50
book $1.00
glue $0.80 Total

8. What fraction is modelled?

9. Yes or No?
Lucy could read 8 pages of a novel in under an hour.

10. Jimmy weighs 35.5 kg. His father is twice as heavy as he is.
What is their total weight?

## Measurement and Geometry

11. Complete these:

(a) 1 h 10 min = minutes

12. Half a kilogram = grams

13. True or False?
This square has an area of 4 cm$^2$.

14. Write mL or L on the containers.

15. What temperature is shown on this thermometer?

0° 25° 50° 75° 100°

16. Complete the table about regular polygons.

| Shape | Pentagon | Hexagon | Nonagon |
|---|---|---|---|
| No. of sides | | | |

17. What prism can be made from this set of faces?

18. Draw a sharp angle inside this circle (use the centre point).

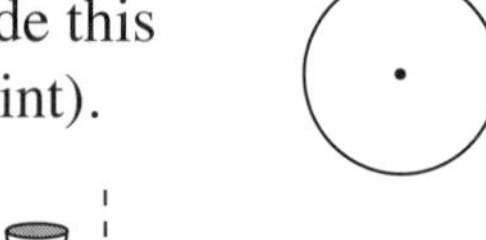

19. Flip this picture over the dotted line.

20. Write the position of the tennis ball.

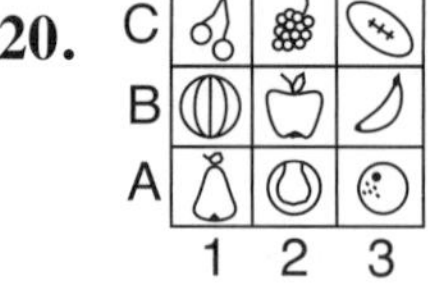


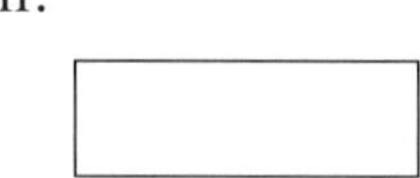

## Statistics and Probability

21. (a) What coin did Mary have the most of?
(b) What was the value of the 5c coins?

Number of Coins: 0, 10, 20, 30, 40, 50
5c 10c 20c 50c $1 $2

(a) (b)

## Adam's Boat

When Granpa and Adam arrived at the boatyard the next day, *Patsy* was being lowered by a big crane into a strange looking wooden cradle. All that day and the next, and the next, Granpa and Adam helped with the hard job of scraping and chipping off *Patsy's* old paint. They wrenched off her rotten timbers and hammered new pieces into place. Adam felt quite important, with all the people looking on.

When *Patsy* was ready they took big paint brushes and slapped on a thick coat of red paint.

Adam was busy with his paintbrush when Mr Barton and Mr James came up to him.

"We know how you feel about *Patsy*," said Mr James. "How would you like it if we gave her a new name? How about—Adam's Boat?"

"You can't do that!" said Adam. "She's Old Ben's boat. Her name is *Patsy*."

"Then *Patsy* she shall be," said Mr Barton. He and Mr James went to paint *Patsy* very carefully in gold letters on each side of her bow.

From *Adam's Boat* by Mary Small

## Reading and Comprehension

1. What purpose did the strange looking wooden cradle serve?
   (a) It was used as a ladder.
   (b) The timber was used to make a dashboard.
   (c) It formed part of the crane.
   (d) It secured the boat into a steady position.

2. Before painting took place, it was necessary to
   (a) give the boat a name.
   (b) scrape off the old paint.
   (c) reverse the crane.
   (d) mix the new colour.

3. What did they end up naming the boat?
   (a) *Old Ben* (b) *Patsy*
   (c) *Adam's Boat* (d) *Mr Barton*

4. Which two colours were used on the boat?

   ______________________________

5. Number these sentences in order (1–4).
   (a) The boat was lowered into place.
   (b) The name was written in gold.
   (c) Rotten timbers were wrenched off.
   (d) It was named *Patsy*.

## Spelling and Vocabulary

Rewrite the misspelt words.

6. Toonite is jazz ballet night.

   ______________________________

7. Aunty May was tyed of washing the soiled nappies. ______________

Circle the word that has the nearest meaning to the underlined word.

8. Aaron's <u>trunk</u> was damaged at the airport.
   (a) treasure chest (b) nose
   (c) case (d) team

9. Sally takes <u>double</u> the time to wash the dishes.
   (a) half (b) twice (c) most (d) two

Circle the correct word in brackets.

10. A (gently, gentle) blow was enough to extinguish the candle.

11. The teacher had to inquire (farther, further) about the fight.

12. The masked person wanted to (steel, steal) the jewels from the cabinet.

## Grammar and Punctuation

13. Underline the **adverbs** in these sentences.

    Sally dropped wearily onto the soft couch. She had been digging busily in the front yard all morning. Slowly Sally sipped her water.

14. Punctuate and capitalise this sentence.

    quite unaware of the danger nicholas the three year old boy walked towards the boat

    ______________________________

    ______________________________

# Mathematics



## Number and Algebra

1.

| + | 9 | 19 | 29 | 39 | 49 | 99 |
|---|---|---|---|---|---|---|
| 2 | | | | | | |

2.

| – | 70 | 60 | 50 | 40 | 30 | 106 |
|---|---|---|---|---|---|---|
| 7 | | | | | | |

3.

| × | 4 | 8 | 10 | 3 | 6 | 11 |
|---|---|---|---|---|---|---|
| 9 | | | | | | |

**4.** Write the numeral for:
7000 + 90 + 4 =

**5.** Write in the missing numbers: 100, 95, 90, ☐, ☐, ☐, 70

**6.** Which is smaller, $1\frac{1}{2}$ or $5\frac{1}{2}$?

**7.** How many $5 notes have the same value as $100?

**8.** Which fraction is the biggest?
0.92, 0.80, 0.43, 0.11

**9.** Tick the best answer.
Maria spent how much at the school tuckshop? $600, $6, $60

**10.** A farmer had 84 sheep but sold 26. How many did he have left?

## Measurement and Geometry

**11.** How many minutes till the next o'clock?

(a) 9:55 (b) 10:45

(c) 2:09

**12.** Complete: (a) 3 kg = ☐ g

(b) 4.5 kg = ☐ g

**13.** Find the area of this shape.

**14.** What is the total volume of this set of shampoo bottles?

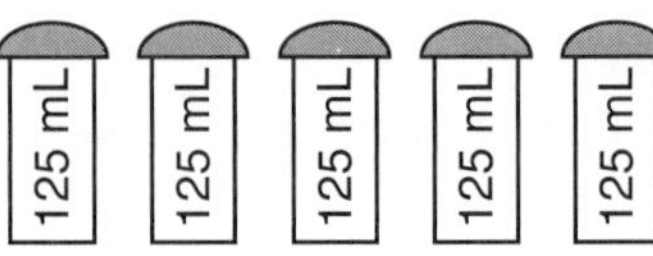


**15.** The temperature on a cold winter's night would be: 40°C, 18°C, 4°C, 27°C

**16.** Which shape below is a polygon?

(a) (b) (c) (d) (e)

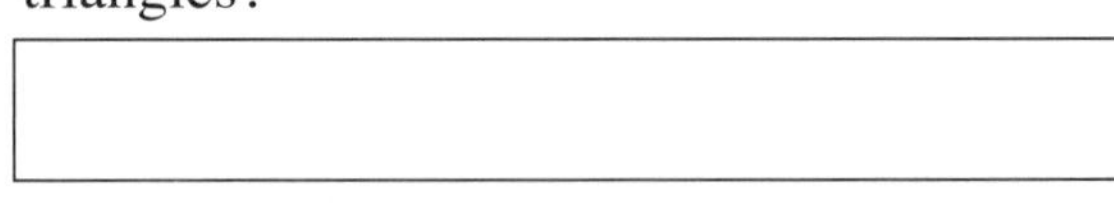

**17.** What pyramid is made from a set of four triangles?

**18.**

These angles are all _ _ _ _ _ _ .

**19.** Does a circle tessellate?

**20.** Shade a combination of 3 petals so that the answer is 15.

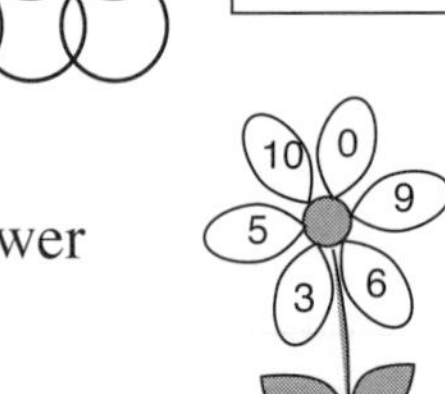


## Statistics and Probability

**21.** Chips
Egg
Ham
Bananas
Bread
5 10 15 20 25 30
kg of Food Eaten

How many more kilograms of bread were eaten than eggs?

## Show Off!

In last year's Grade 5, Amanda Browne won the prize for 'Most Imaginative Creature' in the Art and Craft section. Her entry was a pineapple stuck with toothpicks to look like an echidna. Mrs Black kept mentioning that. "Perhaps this year's Grade 5 will win something too"—she must have said it ten times a day in the week before the show. "Especially since we have Amanda's cousin in our class this year."
Matthew Browne just kept staring at the spider crawling on the windowsill.
Amanda was known for the things she did well. People always remembered Matthew for his mistakes. They remembered when Matthew spilt glue on the gym floor; got stuck in the roof when collecting tennis balls; or fell off the ladder into the Grade 2 herb garden. And they always remembered whose cousin he was.
Saturday was the Valley Show.

From *Show Off* by Hazel Edwards

## Reading and Comprehension

1. What grade is Amanda Browne in this year?
   (a) Grade 4 (b) Grade 5
   (c) Grade 6 (d) Grade 7

2. What was the name of the event that the students were asked to participate in?
   (a) Art and Craft Section
   (b) The Valley Show
   (c) Imaginative Creature
   (d) Grade 5 Competition

3. What was Matthew doing while Mrs Black was explaining the competition details?
   (a) talking
   (b) collecting tennis balls
   (c) spilling glue on the floor
   (d) staring at a spider

4. Name two things that Matthew Browne will always be remembered for.

   ________________________________________

   ________________________________________

5. Number these sentences in order (1–4).
   (a) Saturday was the Valley Show.
   (b) Amanda Browne won the Art and Craft Section.
   (c) Matthew Browne is in the Year 5 class.
   (d) Matthew fell off a ladder.

## Spelling and Vocabulary

Rewrite the misspelt words.

6. Joanna used the left-over pieces of timba to start the fire. ________________

7. Felicity told me that my answer was troo.

   ________________________________________

Circle the word that has the nearest meaning to the underlined word.

8. The animals boarded the Ark, <u>couple</u> by couple.
   (a) twice (b) some (c) lots (d) two

9. Simpson carried the <u>wounded</u> to the First Aid station.
   (a) worried (b) soldiers
   (c) harmful (d) injured

Circle the correct word in brackets.

10. We cleared a (truck, track) through the bush by using a scythe.

11. (Either, Neither) child can take the message to the library.

12. Joanne took her shoes off before (entered, entering) the house.

## Grammar and Punctuation

13. Underline the **verbs** in these sentences.

    Mum opened the front door. The visitor smiled at her. Then he hugged her and gave her the tulips. "Come in," she said.

14. Punctuate and capitalise in this sentence.

    jingle bell rock would have to be my favourite christmas song

    ________________________________________

    ________________________________________

## Number and Algebra

1.

| + | 8 | 15 | 7 | 19 | 2 | 106 |
|---|---|---|---|---|---|---|
| 7 | | | | | | |

2.

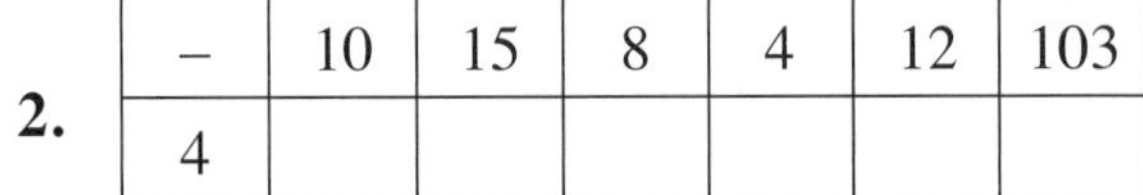

| – | 10 | 15 | 8 | 4 | 12 | 103 |
|---|---|---|---|---|---|---|
| 4 | | | | | | |

3.

| ÷ | 16 | 8 | 56 | 72 | 80 | 96 |
|---|---|---|---|---|---|---|
| 8 | | | | | | |

**4.** Circle the value of the 7 in 6752.
7000, 700, 70 or 7

**5.** Complete the number sequence. 18, 118, 218,

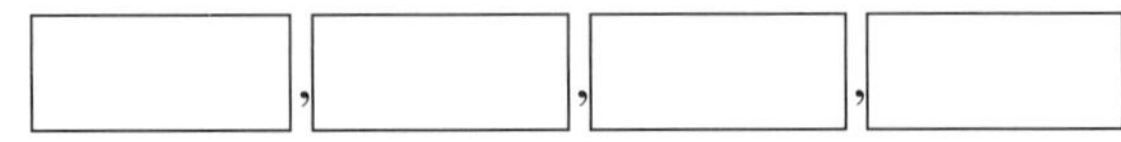

**6.** How many triangles?

**7.** Share these coins with 3 people. How much does each get? 20c 20c 20c

**8.** Complete the labels.

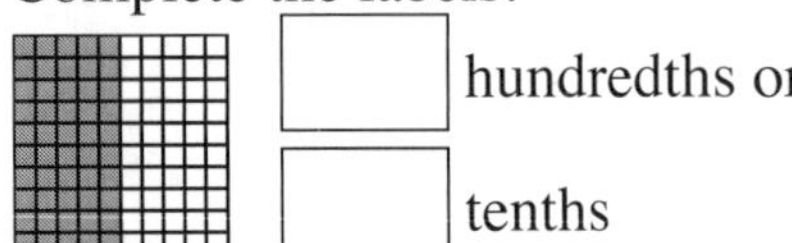

hundredths or

tenths

**9.** Circle the best answer:
My dad's height is 2 m, 2 cm, 2 mm.

**10.** Draw in all the possible paths from the starting stone.

START

## Measurement and Geometry

**11.** Complete these time facts.

(a) ☐ seconds = 1 minute

(b) ☐ days = 1 week

(c) ☐ hours = 1 day

**12.** Colour the weights needed to balance the food item.

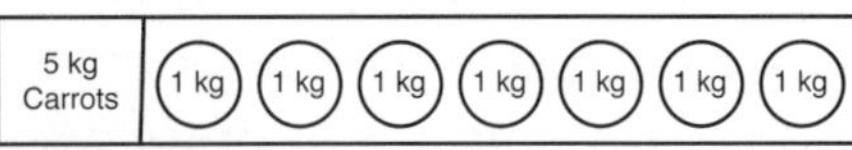


**13.** Find the area of the leaf.

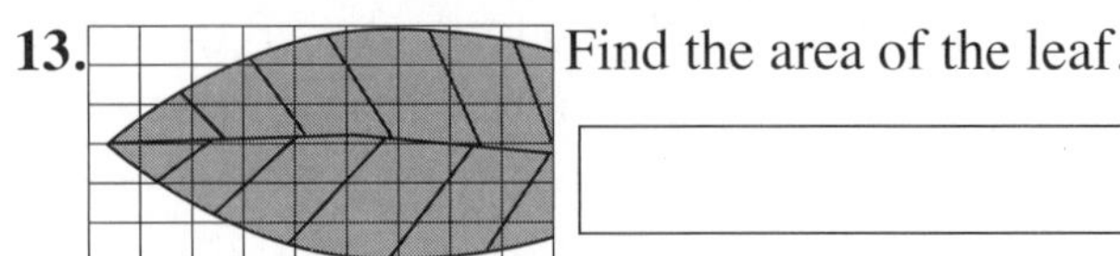

**14.** Would you use L or mL to measure the liquid in a capful of detergent?

**15.** Write a temperature that would have been recorded on a very hot day.

**16.** Look at the frame Cindy made. How many pairs of sides are parallel?

**17.** Draw in the faces which make up a square pyramid.

**18.** These angles all look:

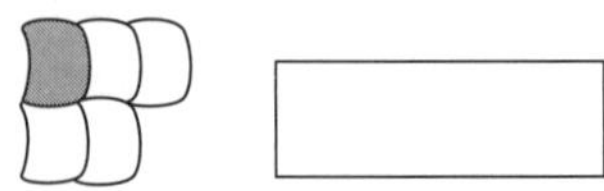

**19.** Does the coloured shape tessellate?

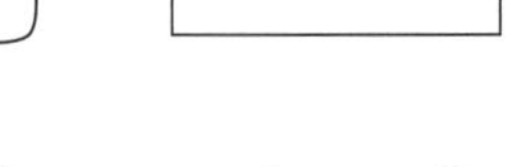

**20.** Draw a broken line from the triangle to the circle.

## Statistics and Probability

**21.**

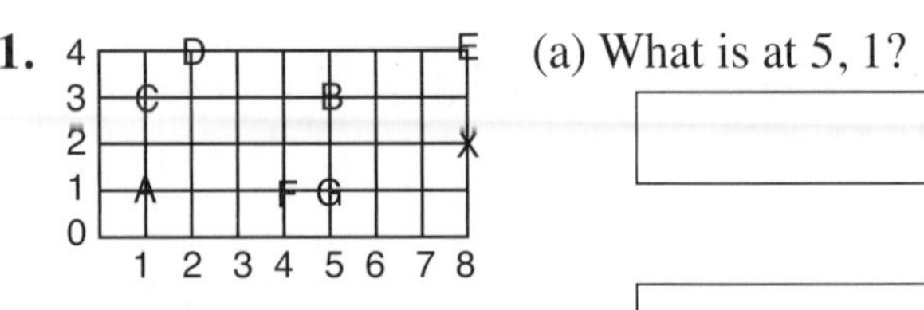


(a) What is at 5, 1?

(b) What is in position 8, 2?

## Premier to Fly North Today

The Premier, Sir Bill Kytes, will fly to North Queensland today to inspect the damage done by Cyclone Brunella.

Sir Bill Kytes will visit the worst affected areas of Malanda, Tully, Innisfail and Ingham. "It's important for me to witness the situation so that the State Government can move promptly through its Disaster Relief Program."

Food drops and damage assessment are already underway and the Federal Government has promised to assist sugar cane and banana growers, whose plantations have been damaged by the cyclonic conditions. "It's crucial that the State Government gets an accurate picture of the total damage, before any finance is given," said a Government representative early yesterday morning.

"We know we need to act hastily because many parts are blacked out due to fallen power lines. Most towns are inaccessible and unfortunately three lives have already been lost."

## Reading and Comprehension

**1.** Which word in the article means 'not being easily reached'?

(a) accurate (b) promptly
(c) inaccessible (d) disastrous

**2.** What was the cause of the blacked-out areas?

(a) poor banana plantations
(b) fallen power lines
(c) too much rain
(d) not enough money

**3.** Circle the adjective form of the word *cyclone*.

(a) cyclones (b) cyclonically
(c) cyclonic (d) cyclometer

**4.** (a) Write the name of the Premier.

______________________________

(b) Write the name of the cyclone.

______________________________

**5.** Number these sentences in order (1–4).

(a) Food drops are already underway.
(b) Unfortunately three lives have been lost.
(c) The Premier will fly to North Queensland.
(d) The worst off areas were towns like Tully and Ingham.

## Spelling and Vocabulary

Rewrite the misspelt words.

**6.** To me, a screaming baby is an uglee sight.

______________________________

**7.** Patrick rushed upsdares to turn off the light.

______________________________

Choose the word that has the nearest meaning to the underlined word.

**8.** Billy was <u>wrong</u> in thinking Allan had done it.

(a) mistaken (b) right (c) cross (d) willing

**9.** The <u>proper</u> thing to do was stand up for the pensioner.

(a) perfect (b) decent
(c) good (d) nice

Circle the correct word in brackets.

**10.** Travis didn't mean to (spilt, spill) the beans about the celebration.

**11.** The (forth, fourth) child to leave the room was Samantha Hogan.

**12.** I tried to (forgot, forget) about the immunisation I received yesterday.

## Grammar and Punctuation

**13.** Underline the **nouns** in these sentences.

Jan looked really pretty in her new dress and leather shoes. She bought them on Tuesday at Tylers.

**14.** Punctuate and capitalise this sentence.

on my table is a box filled with paper crayons glue tinsel and foam pieces

______________________________

______________________________

## Number and Algebra

1. Complete this addition grid.

| + | 1 | 2 | 3 | 4 | 5 |
|---|---|---|---|---|---|
| 6 | | | | | |
| 7 | | | | | |
| 8 | | | | | |
| 9 | | | | | |

2. Complete this subtraction ladder.

| 21 | 19 | 17 | | | | | | | |
|---|---|---|---|---|---|---|---|---|---|

3. Follow this multiplication path.

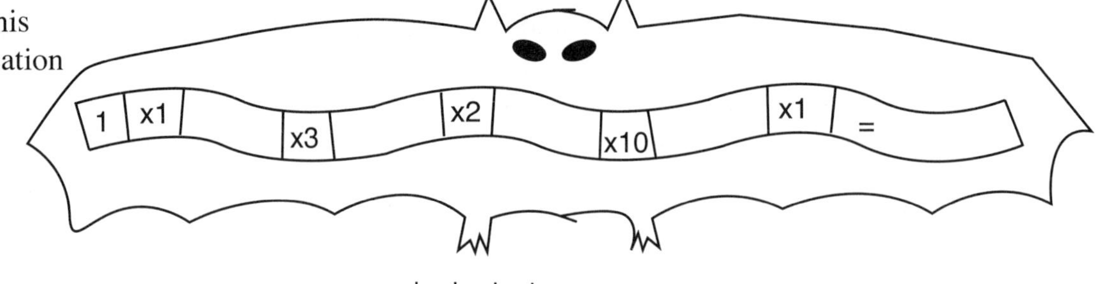


4. Write the numeral shown on the abacus.

Th H T U

5. Complete these sequences.

(a) 1980, 1880, 1780, ____, ____, ____

(b) 10 000, 9000, 8000, ____, ____, ____

6. Complete each label.

(a)

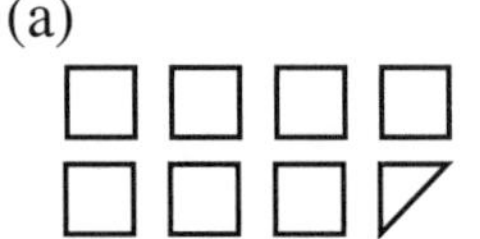

____ and a half

(b)

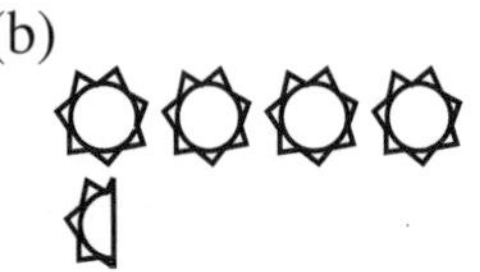

____ and a half

(c)

____ and a half

(d)

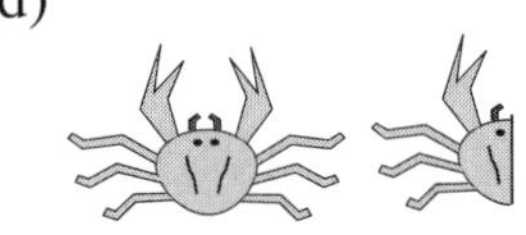

____ and a half

7. How many $50 notes have the same value as: (a) $500 ____ (b) $250 ____ (c) $150 ____

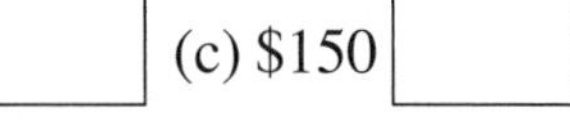

8. Write the decimal fraction for the part not coloured.

(a)

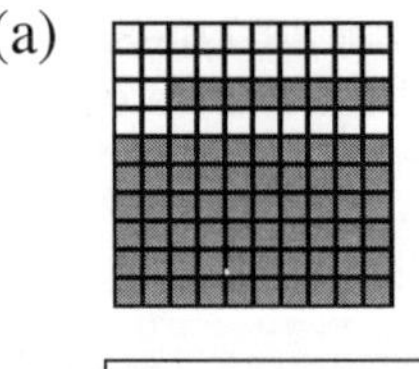

(b)

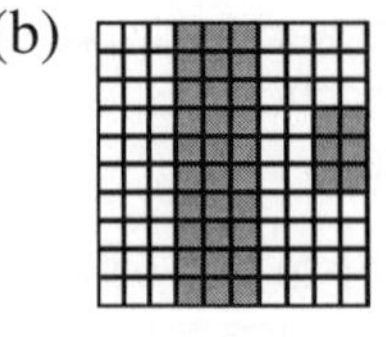

(c)

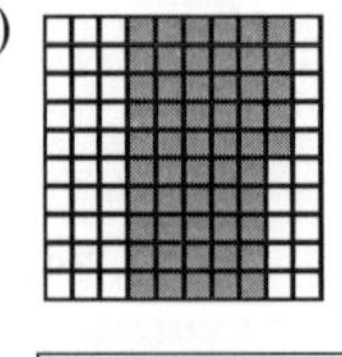

(d)

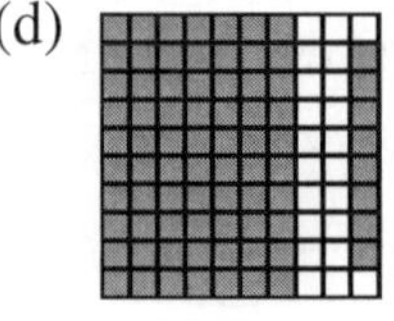

(e)

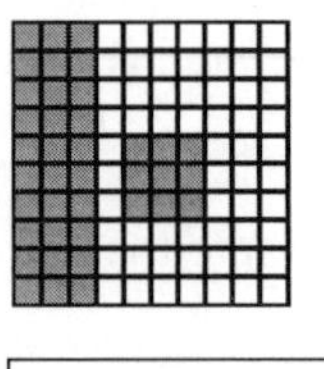

9. Give the multiple of 100 that is closest to each number below.

(a) 184 ____ (b) 209 ____ (c) 3 401 ____ (d) 97 ____ (e) 486 ____

10. A dressmaker bought 20 metres of silk material. She made seven dresses, each of which used 2 metres of material. How much silk did she have left over?

## Measurement and Geometry

11. Show these times on the analogue clocks. (a) 6:55  (b) 3:20 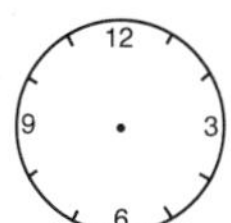

12. Draw a horizontal line five centimetres long.
Find half-way and label the point A.
Trace over this line in blue pencil.

13. On the grid, draw a polygon with an area of 8 squares.

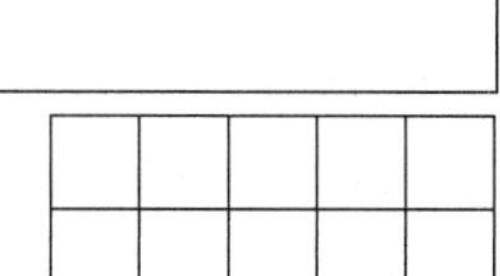

14. What is the total volume of this letter model if each block has sides 1 cm?

15. On each thermometer, colur the mercury to match the temperature given.

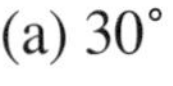

(a) 30° (b) 18° (c) 6°

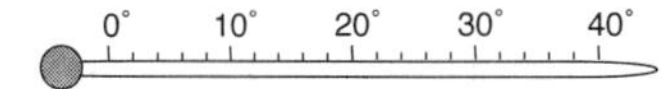

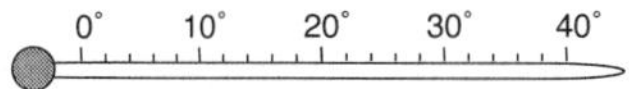


16. Complete this statement. A square has ☐ lines of symmetry.

17. Complete this statement. A cube has ☐ faces, ☐ vertices and ☐ edges.

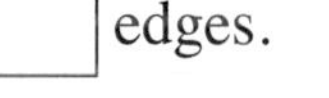

18. Write these angles in order of size. (a)  (b) 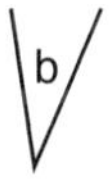 (c) 

19. Put a cross on the pictures that show flip, colour the ones that show slide, and circle those that show turn.

(a)   (b)  (c)   (d)   (e) 

20.

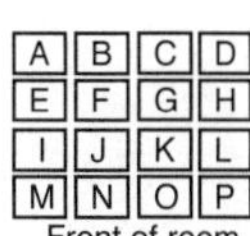


(a) Shelley is sitting at desk L. She moves 3 desks to the left, then 1 desk forward. Where is she now?

(b) Joshua is sitting at desk C. He moves 2 desks forward, then 1 desk to the right. Where is he now?

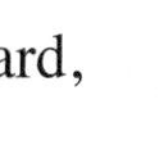

## Statistics and Probability

21. 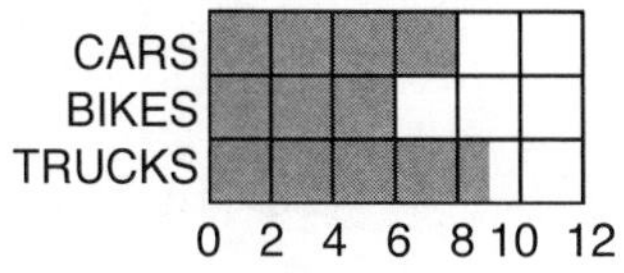 CARS / BIKES / TRUCKS (bar graph, scale 0 2 4 6 8 10 12)

How many vehicles passed our school gate altogether?

## D-DAY (Doomsday)

I feel sick! I think I'm getting a serious migraine. My foot hurts from softball practice on Tuesday morning. Mum said I can ring her if I feel like vomiting. Wonder what a migraine is? My stomach has a funny pain. It's more in the middle than on the right-hand side. I know I'm coming down with the flu. I'm not too sure, but it could be insomnia. No, that's not right, you can only get insomnia in your foot.

I bolted down the side driveway, raced inside and, as usual, Mum and Dad were in the shop serving customers. I went straight to my room and just stood there staring at myself in the mirror. Are my teeth green? I felt ab-so-lu-tely miserable. I felt like bawling. This has to be, without a shadow of a doubt, the worst day of my entire Year 6 life. I wiped the tears away with my black baggy sports shorts.

Just look at me. I feel awful. I DO look like the 'Incredible Sulk'.

You see, this is how I honestly reacted to my next Social Studies assignment. My teacher, Miss BOSSYROONY, gave us a new project today, which has to be finished within the next fortnight.

She said: "Class, I'd like you all to do a project on Australia's immigration and how, in … blah blah blah … Australia … blah blah blah … Australia is a multicultural … blah blah blah … and many migrants have … blah blah blah … here. Please don't forget to include a map, and it would be lovely if the pictures could be … blah blah blah …"

We all stared at Miss Bossyroony and then looked at each other right in the mince pies.

"Is this woman for real?" I whispered to Rebecca. "She IS joking, right?" I asked again.

I looked at Miss B long and hard. I think she's gone a bit 'blah blah' herself.

It was then that I was given 200 lines on classroom manners. I'm sick of orders, I thought to myself.

Yep, yep, this next project was a real beauty—absolutely impossible!

## Reading and Comprehension

1. The child in the extract didn't feel well because she
   (a) had the flu.
   (b) was working in the shop.
   (c) didn't like her teacher.
   (d) was given another project.

2. *Mince pies* refer to
   (a) the eyes.
   (b) the small pies.
   (c) the migrants from European countries.
   (d) Rebecca's nickname.

3. This was a Grade ______ classroom.
   (a) 7
   (b) 6
   (c) 5
   (d) 2

4. What does *multicultural* mean?

   ____________________________________

   ____________________________________

5. Number these sentences in order (1–4).
   (a) I don't think I can do this!
   (b) I felt really sick this morning.
   (c) I was given a Social Studies assignment.
   (d) It is about Australia's immigration.

## Spelling and Vocabulary

Rewrite these sentences, correcting the misspelt words.

6. I'm not shore what the word imigration means so I'll cheque it in the dictionery.

   ____________________________________

   ____________________________________

7. I did feel mizrable. I felt like balling.

   ____________________________________

   ____________________________________

Which word has the same, or nearly the same, meaning as the word underlined?

8. I ran into my room <u>bawling</u> because Dad yelled at me.
   (a) bellowing
   (b) crying
   (c) baby
   (d) bowling

9. I felt a bit <u>restless</u> about this new school assignment.
   (a) tired
   (b) awful
   (c) uneasy
   (d) wrong

Circle the word in brackets which is the best fit for the sentence.

10. Many (immigration, migrants) have come to our country.

11. I have tasted food and drink from many (cultural, cultures).

12. Immigration is not something that just happened in the (past, passed).

## Grammar and Punctuation

13. Underline the **prepositions** in these sentences.

    I bolted down the driveway. Mum and Dad were in the shop serving Mr and Mrs Rowlinson. I raced towards the lolly counter and snuck out the back door.

14. Rewrite this sentence with correct punctuation and capitalisation.

    help i think im getting a migraine now

    ____________________________________

    ____________________________________

## Number and Algebra

1.

| + | 3 | 7 | 4 | 6 | 8 | 67 |
|---|---|---|---|---|---|---|
| 9 | | | | | | |

2.

| – | 10 | 15 | 13 | 20 | 19 | 67 |
|---|---|---|---|---|---|---|
| 9 | | | | | | |

3.

| × | 1 | 5 | 8 | 9 | 10 | 15 |
|---|---|---|---|---|---|---|
| 9 | | | | | | |

4. Write the numeral for: 1000 + 100 + 1

5. Complete this number pattern.
fifteen hundredths, twenty hundredths,
twenty-five hundredths, ______, ______, ______

6. Make 4 shares.
one share =
left over =

7. What is the least number of notes needed to make $25?

8. Write in decimal form:
(a) 2 and 75 hundredths
(b) 4 and 12 hundredths

9. True or False? Most classes would have at least 50 students.

10. Draw in the dot pattern for D. (These are triangular numbers)

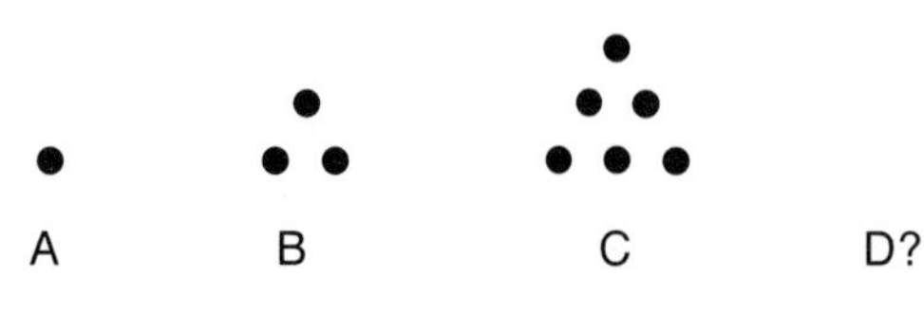


## Measurement and Geometry

11. Show 38 minutes past 10 on this clock.

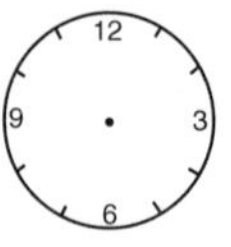


12. True or false? 3000 g is equal to 3 kg.

13. What is the area of this rectangle in square centimetres?

14. Give the volume of this model.

15. Circle the 3 hot temperatures listed below.
90°C, 70°C, 85°C, 20°C

16. Look at the rhombus frame Celine made.
(a) How many equal sides are there?
(b) How many pairs of opposite sides are equal?

17. What could this shape be a top view of?

18. Shade the sharpest angle.

19. Slide this bar of soap to the right.

20. Give directions for the cat to get to the apple tree.

## Statistics and Probability

21. On a picture graph, 옷 represents 5 people. How many figures will be needed for 15 people?

## Luxurious Property Comes with Plenty of Extras

This luxurious house comes with a full-size tennis court. The vendors, who have recently finished building this superb property, have put it on the market due to a work transfer.

Marble of different colours has been used extensively in the downstairs living areas. The house has high ceilings throughout, with wide double doors to the main entry. The main bedroom has an ensuite with a spa and massive walk-in robe.

The spacious kitchen has granite benchtops and outside there is a special Asian cooking area which runs on gas burners.

The property has other fine inclusions, like air conditioners in all the bedrooms, alarm system, dishwasher, vacuumaid, and a computerised sprinkler system. Marketing agent Derwin Josler of Norton Realty says it is for sale by negotiation.

To arrange an inspection, phone Derwin on 3666 5336 or 0417 290 566.

## Reading and Comprehension

1. Vendors are also referred to as
   (a) agents. (b) sellers.
   (c) buyers. (d) builders.

2. Why is the house being sold?
   (a) The owners are sick of it.
   (b) The tennis court is difficult to maintain.
   (c) The owners got a job transfer.
   (d) The ceilings are too high.

3. This home is open for inspection
   (a) on weekends only.
   (b) by negotiation.
   (c) by ringing the real estate agent.
   (d) when the vendors finish building.

4. List three extras this house includes.

   ______________________________

   ______________________________

   ______________________________

5. Number these sentences in order (1–4).
   (a) The main bedroom has an ensuite.
   (b) Ring Norton Realty for an inspection.
   (c) The marketing agent is Mr Josler.
   (d) This special property includes a tennis court.

## Spelling and Vocabulary

Rewrite the misspelt words.

6. I thought the surprise party was a tremendous idear. ______________

7. My nanna has a blue ellektrik blanket.

   ______________________________

Circle the word that has the nearest meaning to the underlined word.

8. My uncle had to take down the <u>minutes</u> of the meeting.
   (a) money (b) record
   (c) time (d) message

9. The teacher <u>grasped</u> the opportunity to punish the child.
   (a) seized (b) grab
   (c) got (d) held

Circle the correct word in brackets.

10. From the (noise, noisy) room came the six-year-old girl.

11. The (juice, juicy) grapes were placed in a bowl in the fridge.

12. Kirk doesn't know (weather, whether) to invite you or not.

## Grammar and Punctuation

13. Underline the **nouns** in these sentences.

    The man who lives next door to us owns a computer business. He started in January and has made a lot of money.

14. Punctuate and capitalise this sentence.

    the qantas jumbo landed at half past eleven

    ______________________________

    ______________________________

## Number and Algebra

1.

| + | 7 | 3 | 9 | 12 | 5 | 76 |
|---|---|---|---|---|---|---|
| 4 | | | | | | |

2.

| – | 13 | 15 | 11 | 18 | 16 | 72 |
|---|---|---|---|---|---|---|
| 4 | | | | | | |

3.

| ÷ | 24 | 4 | 0 | 16 | 40 | 100 |
|---|---|---|---|---|---|---|
| 4 | | | | | | |

4. What number is made up of 6 thousands, 3 hundreds and 2 ones?

5. Complete the sequence.

0.9, 0.8, 0.7, ____, ____, ____

6. Make three shares.

one share =

left over =

7. How many \$50 notes have the same value as \$350?

8. Complete the label to show the part not coloured.

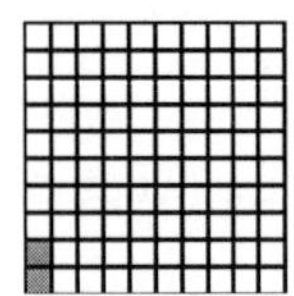

9. True or False? The average family has three cars.

10. Place the numbers 1 to 5 in the five squares so that any three numbers in a row add up to the same number.

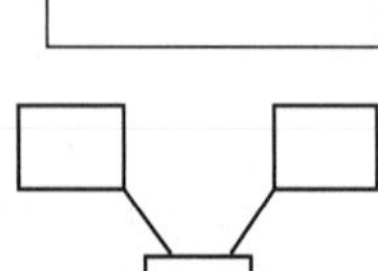

## Measurement and Geometry

11. Show sixteen minutes past three on this digital watch.

:

12. True or False? 500 cm is equal to 50 m.

13. Draw a rectangle with an area of six square centimetres.

14. What is the capacity of this model?

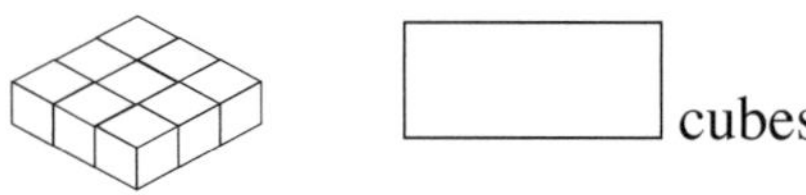


15. Circle the lowest temperature.
13°C, 80°C, 23°C

16. A shape with only one pair of parallel sides is called a _ _ _ p _ _ _ _ _ m .

17. What am I?
I have a square base and 4 triangular faces.

18. What type of angles have been made?

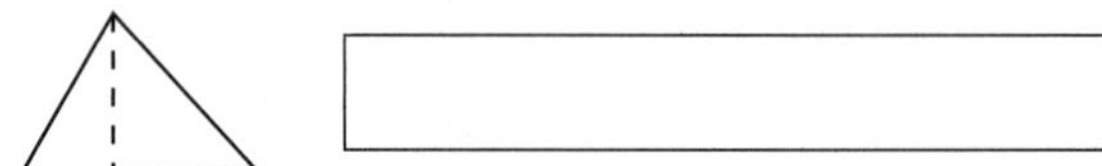

19. Turn the umbrella in an anticlockwise direction.

20. ✔ ✔ ✔ ✔ ✔ ✔ ✔ ✔ ✔ ✔
Circle the third tick, and underline the fifth one.

## Statistics and Probability

21. Finish the column graph using the data.

| *Name* | *No. of Stickers* |
|---|---|
| Kia | 6 |
| Carl | 2 |
| Ben | 7 |
| Tom | 3 |
| Jim | 4 |

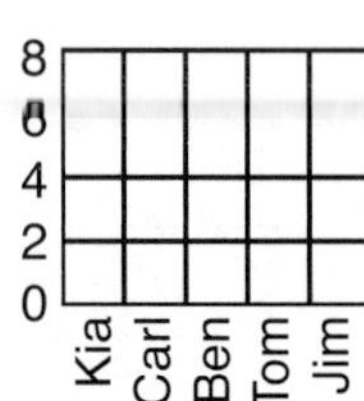

## Going Fishing with My Dad

During the next week I weeded the garden and pestered Dad to take me fishing. I washed the car and pestered Dad to take me fishing. I tidied the garage and pestered Dad to take me fishing.

"All right," he said at last, worn down by my persistence. "I'll take you fishing this Sunday, but only if you promise not to help me anymore."

He said that because I had pulled out his precious bird's-nest fern, smeared the windscreen of the new car and spilt nuts and bolts all over the garage floor (accidentally, of course!). I didn't care. My dad was taking me fishing!

On Sunday morning the sky looked black. Dad was sitting at the table eating cornflakes. He didn't look happy.

I heard Mum say, "You did promise to take him fishing! A promise is a promise." In other words, if you promise something you should do it—no matter what. (Thanks Mum!)

Dad didn't answer. He looked as though he wanted to go back to bed.

I wouldn't let him, though. No way! Not after I'd done all that work! We drove off, then hired a motor boat, and by ten o'clock we were sitting in the middle of a big river, ready to begin our day of great fun.

From *Going Fishing with My Dad* by Jan Weeks

## Reading and Comprehension

**1.** The second chore done to change Dad's mind about fishing was
(a) weeding the garden.
(b) washing the car.
(c) tidying the garage.
(d) cleaning the bird's nest.

**2.** What was Dad doing on the morning of the fishing trip?
(a) cleaning the bolts off the garage floor
(b) washing the windscreen
(c) sitting, eating cornflakes
(d) sleeping in bed—again

**3.** *Persistence* means
(a) 'proper'. (b) 'promise'.
(c) 'pestering'. (d) 'perseverance'.

**4.** What time did they arrive at the river? ____________________

**5.** Number these sentences in order (1–4).
(a) On Sunday the weather was awful.
(b) We drove to the river.
(c) I did all these chores for Dad.
(d) Dad said that he'd take me fishing.

## Spelling and Vocabulary

Rewrite the misspelt words.

**6.** The only thing that cheared me up was my dad's joke. ____________________

**7.** Dosnt it bother you that you're going to be late? ____________________

Circle the word that has the nearest meaning to the underlined word.

**8.** That small puppy <u>relies</u> a great deal on its mother.
(a) cried (b) depends
(c) ran (d) relished

**9.** Father <u>forgot</u> to post my letter this morning.
(a) flew (b) remembered
(c) failed (d) knew

Circle the correct word in brackets.

**10.** Dad gets (payed, paid) on the last Wednesday of the month.

**11.** (Aern't, Aren't, Aunt) you going to wash the apple first?

**12.** The shoes (coast, cost) me nineteen dollars and ninety-five cents.

## Grammar and Punctuation

**13.** Underline the **verbs** in these sentences.

The boys divided their marbles fairly. We all checked our share by counting. I tossed my marbles into a bag.

**14.** Punctuate and capitalise this sentence.

my aunty beth wasnt sure whether to choose the orange peach lime or pink scarf

____________________

____________________

## Number and Algebra

**1.**

| + | 7 | 1 | 5 | 9 | 3 | 98 |
|---|---|---|---|---|---|---|
| 10 | | | | | | |

**2.**

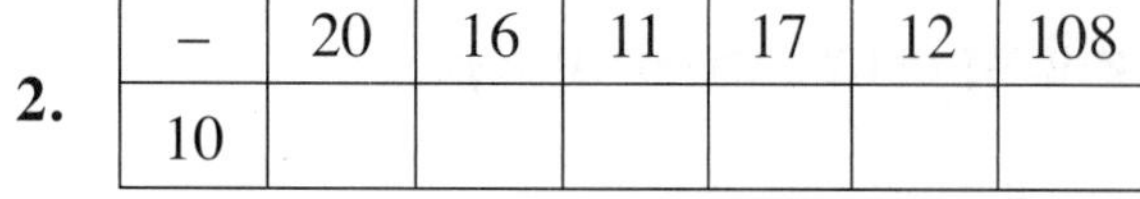

| – | 20 | 16 | 11 | 17 | 12 | 108 |
|---|---|---|---|---|---|---|
| 10 | | | | | | |

**3.**

| × | 10 | 7 | 6 | 0 | 1 | 15 |
|---|---|---|---|---|---|---|
| 10 | | | | | | |

**4.** Write the value of the bold digit in **3**682.

**5.** Fill in the missing numbers: 0.90, 0.89,

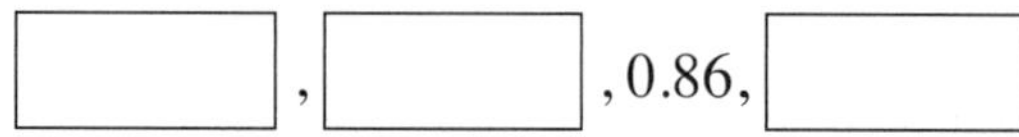

___ , ___ , 0.86, ___

**6.** Share these among five people.

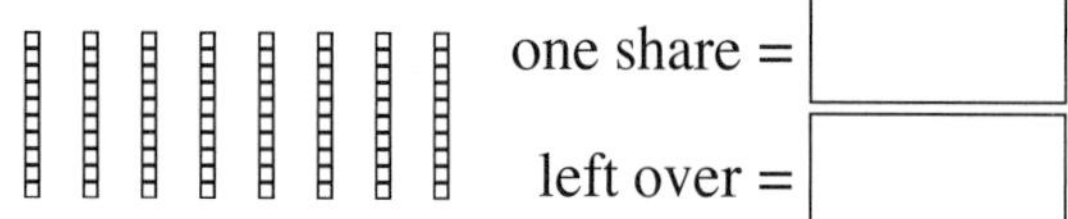

one share =

left over =

**7.** Write these in words. (a) $32 (b) $87.15

(a)

(b)

**8.** Write the decimal fraction for 3 and 33 hundredths.

**9.** True or False?
Most Year 4 children can jog on the spot for over 30 seconds.

**10.** Solve this problem by putting in the correct signs. 5 ☐ 1 = 5

## Measurement and Geometry

**11.** Write the time that is two minutes after:

(a) 5:20 (b) 12:36

**12.** Write these in centimetres.

(a) 1 m 25 cm

(b) 4 m 8 cm

**13.** Find the area of this shape.

**14.** What is the total capacity of these containers?

= ☐ L

**15.** At 11 o'clock today the temperature was 36°C. At 12 o'clock it was 40°C. What is the temperature difference between the two readings?

**16.** A quadrilateral with two pairs of parallel sides can be called a
p _ _ _ _ _ e _ _ g _ _ m .

**17.** Which solid shape has a curved surface, and no corners or edges?

**18.** Draw a straight angle and label it angle S.

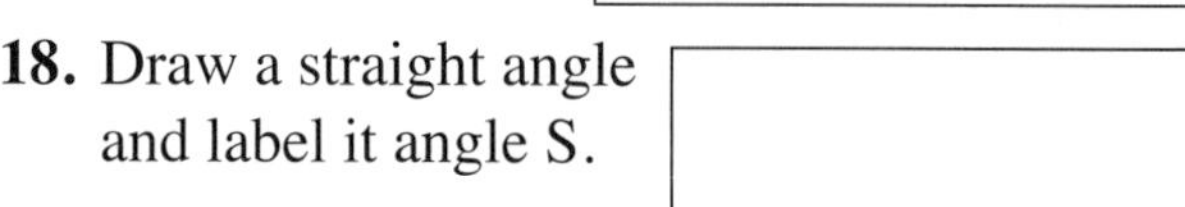

**19.** Is this a good example of flip, turn or slide?

**20.** Finish off the points on this compass.

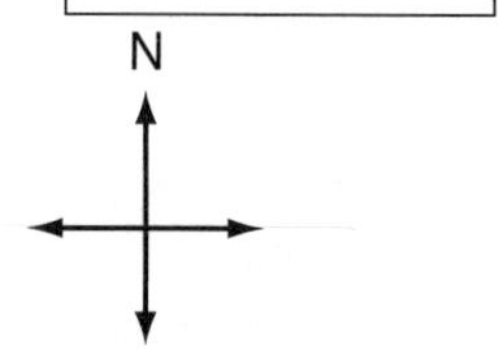


## Statistics and Probability

**21.** Thomas has 14 red marbles, 6 blue and 8 yellow. Complete this column graph.

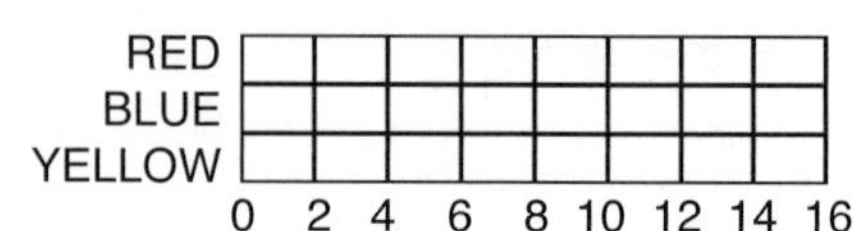

## From the Land of Ikaros

Can someone really fly without an aeroplane? People only fly on television, like Astro Boy. Kosmas loved to hear his Yaya tell the story ...

Ikaros and his father Dedalos were prisoners of the powerful King Minos. He had imprisoned them in a labyrinth.

Dedalos was the most skilled inventor of his time. He had built the labyrinth himself, but now even he did not know the way out of the maze. There was no escape.

The labyrinth had no roof. Day after day, Dedalos gazed at the sky trying to think of a way out. One day, as he watched some birds flying overhead, he suddenly had an idea. *If birds can fly, so can we*, he thought.

Dedalos made two pairs of wings out of feathers and wax. Dedalos and Ikaros strapped the wings on to their shoulders and arms.

When the time came for them to escape, Dedalos warned Ikaros: "Whatever you do, you must not fly too close to the sun or the sea."

Then at last they flapped their wings and rose out of the labyrinth. They flew high into the sky and out over the sea. They were free.

From *From the Land of Ikaros* by Petro Alexiou

## Reading and Comprehension

**1.** This olden-day story is a tale about
(a) Yaya's life in Greece.
(b) the TV character Astro Boy.
(c) Ikaros and Dedalos.
(d) how birds learnt to fly.

**2.** The labyrinth was like a
(a) maze which is difficult to get out of.
(b) laboratory surrounded by huge birds.
(c) modern-day brick prison.
(d) roof of a large house.

**3.** What was the only solution to getting out of the labyrinth?
(a) watch (b) cry
(c) fly (d) dig

**4.** Why did Dedalos warn his son never to fly too close to the sun or the sea?

_______________________________

**5.** Number these sentences in order (1–4).
(a) Dedalos watched some birds fly overhead.
(b) He built two pairs of wings.
(c) Yaya told Kosmas a story of Greek mythology.
(d) Ikaros and Dedalos were King Minos's prisoners.

## Spelling and Vocabulary

Rewrite the misspelt words.

**6.** The young child lernt his manners from his parents. _______________

**7.** The pizza was prepared in a real hurrie.

_______________________________

Circle the word that has the nearest meaning to the word underlined.

**8.** The spider crawled up the chain and frightened me.
(a) afraid (b) followed
(c) scared (d) bit

**9.** The face Grandma pulled was quite funny.
(a) comical (b) scary (c) magic (d) fun

Circle the correct word in brackets.

**10.** The sparrow sitting on the grass has just hurt (it's, its ) wing.

**11.** I (wonder, wander) what I'm getting for Christmas this year!

**12.** We weren't allowed to eat our lunches on the (grass, grassy) area.

## Grammar and Punctuation

**13.** Underline the **adjectives** in these sentences.

The brass bed cost a lot of money, so I bought the wooden one instead. Mum saw the striped quilt she liked. I found two soft pillows.

**14.** Punctuate and capitalise this sentence.

the box that timmy found was addressed to mrs k logan 34 beans rd ascot

_______________________________

_______________________________

## Number and Algebra

1.

| + | 15 | 6 | 13 | 7 | 9 | 55 |
|---|---|---|---|---|---|---|
| 5 | | | | | | |

2.

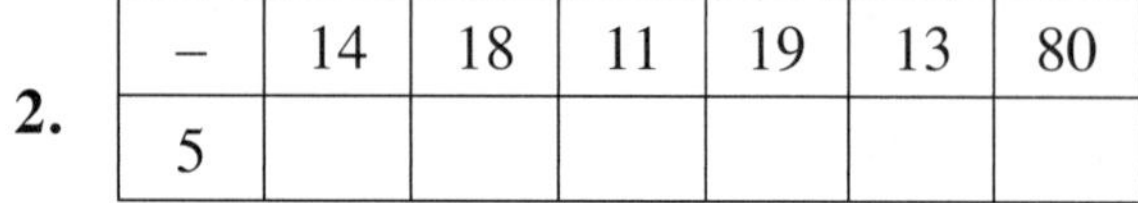

| – | 14 | 18 | 11 | 19 | 13 | 80 |
|---|---|---|---|---|---|---|
| 5 | | | | | | |

3.

| ÷ | 50 | 30 | 10 | 20 | 15 | 100 |
|---|---|---|---|---|---|---|
| 5 | | | | | | |

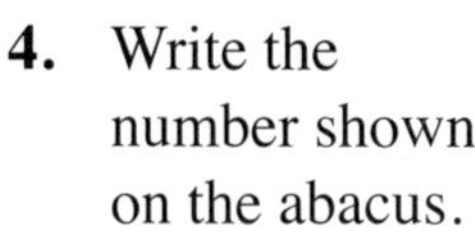

4. Write the number shown on the abacus.

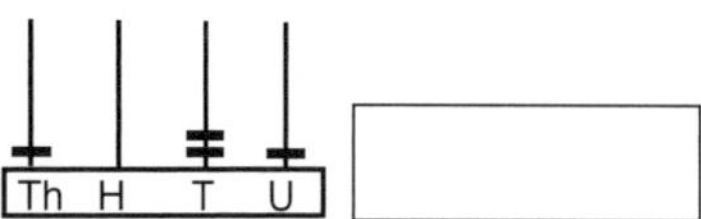


5. Complete this pattern: 0.5, 1, 1.5,

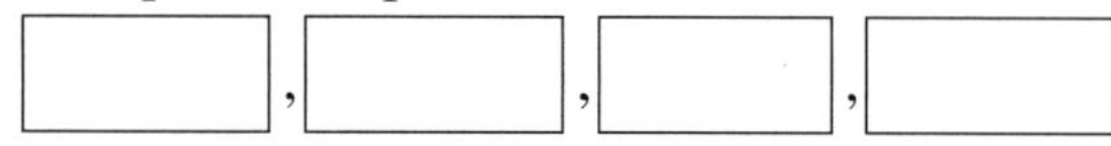

6. Complete this label.

teardrops

7. For each amount, how many people could be given 20 cents?

(a) 60c (b) $2

8. Match the correct fraction.

(1) 2 tens 1 hundredth (a) 0.95
(2) 4 tens 3 hundredths (b) 0.21
(3) 9 tens 5 hundredths (c) 0.43

9. Select the best estimate.
There are about 5, 15, 25 days in a week.

10. How much money have I spent if I used up two fifty dollar notes, a five dollar note and a two dollar coin?

## Measurement and Geometry

11. Find all the 'time' words you can in this puzzle.

| P | A | F | H | M | O |
|---|---|---|---|---|---|
| A | X | A | J | K | L |
| S | E | C | O | N | D |
| T | B | E | N | L | V |

12. Alison is 152 cm tall. Write her height another way.

13. What is the area of this shape in square centimetres?

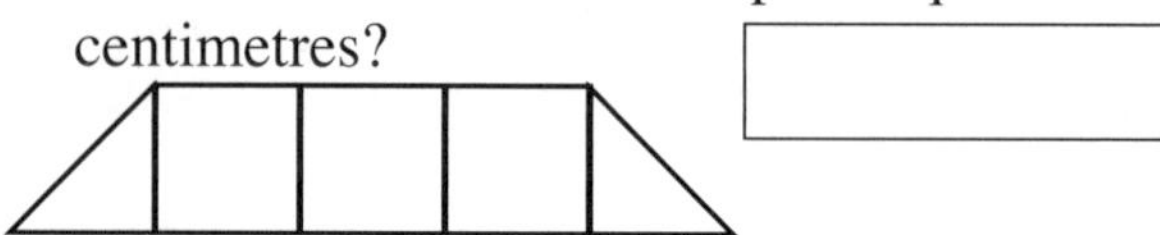

14. What is the total capacity of these containers?

200 mL 200 mL 200 mL 200 mL

15. This illustration suggests a low temperature. Make up a symbol of your own.

16. Measure the length of the sides of this triangle. What do you notice?

17. Yes or No? A rectangular prism has 6 rectangular faces and all its angles are 90°.

18. What type of angle is shaded?

A B C D

19. Draw a picture of a kite. Now flip it over.

20. Draw a teacup in the box. Draw a spoon to the right. Draw a sugar cube in the cup.

## Statistics and Probability

21. $25 $20 $15 $10 $5 $0
SUE KRIS HARRY NG KEN

(a) How much money does Harry have?

(b) Who has $25?

## Delving into the Dictionary

**ticket**—tickets
1. Printed card or paper issued in return for money and giving person right of entry.
2. Tag, a price ticket (N)

**tide**—tides
Rising and falling of the sea (N)

**tidy**—tidies, tidied, tidying, tidier, tidiest (adj.), tidily (adv.)
1. Make neat (verb) *Tidy your room please Lee!*
2. Neat (adj.) *Simone is a tidy worker.*

**tiger**—tigers
A large, wild, striped animal of the cat family (N)

**tight**—tighter, tightest (adj.), tightly (adv.)
1. Fitting close to the body. 2. Stretched.

**tin**—tins
1. Soft white metal (N)
2. Small metal container (N). *A tin of stewed fruit.*

**tiny**—tinier, tiniest (adj.)
Very small.

**tire**—tires, tired, tiring
Grow bored or weary. (verb)

**title**—titles
1. Name of book, movie. (N)
2. Word used before person's name to show rank or position. (N)

**to**
*Sally is going to the beach.* (prep.)

**today**
On this day.
1. *Today is my birthday.* (N) 2. *Come today!* (adv.)

## Reading and Comprehension

1. Give the adverb form of the word *tidy*.
   (a) tidies (b) tidying
   (c) tidily (d) tidied
2. Which word also means 'stretched'?
   (a) title (b) pulled
   (c) neat (d) tight
3. The only verbs on the dictionary page are
   (a) to, today. (b) tight, tiger.
   (c) tin, title. (d) tire, tidy.
4. Put the correct form of *tidy* in this sentence.
   Out of the four of us, Pauline is by far the

   ______________________________ .

5. Number these words into alphabetical order (1–6).
   (a) today (b) ticket (c) tire
   (d) tight (e) tin (f) tides

## Spelling and Vocabulary

Rewrite the misspelt words.

6. Your nee connects the thigh to the lower leg.

   ______________________________

7. Did Captain James Cook discover the east cost of Australia? ____________

Circle the word that has the nearest meaning to the underlined word.

8. The train <u>departed</u> about fifteen minutes ago.
   (a) left (b) boarded
   (c) arrived (d) developed
9. Our class went on an excursion into Brisbane <u>City</u> today.
   (a) sight (b) area
   (c) cities (d) town

Circle the correct word in brackets.

10. The baby (choose, chose) the teddy bear instead of the doll.
11. I knew I had to be ready to hit the ball after (strike, struck) two.
12. At the moment Dad is (spraying, spreying) the lawn with weed killer.

## Grammar and Punctuation

13. Underline the **adverbs** in these sentences.

    She dances merrily on her toes. We looked everywhere for the tambourine. I was once this young.

14. Punctuate and capitalise this sentence.

    on 2nd november we shall be competing in the gold coast walkathon

    ______________________________

    ______________________________

## Number and Algebra

1.

| + | 7 | 6 | 9 | 14 | 3 | 106 |
|---|---|---|---|---|---|---|
| 6 | | | | | | |

2.

| – | 16 | 12 | 15 | 9 | 11 | 105 |
|---|---|---|---|---|---|---|
| 6 | | | | | | |

3.

| × | 3 | 8 | 2 | 9 | 10 | 15 |
|---|---|---|---|---|---|---|
| 6 | | | | | | |

4. Write the number shown by the blocks.

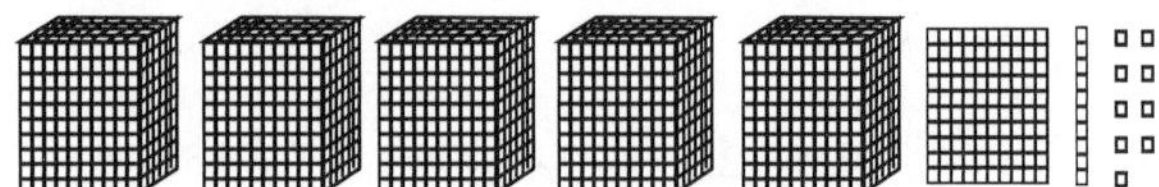

5. Complete this sequence: 6, 12, 18, ___, ___, 36, ___, ___

6. Circle the smallest fraction of each pair.
(a) $8\frac{1}{2}$ or $9\frac{1}{2}$ (b) $3\frac{1}{2}$ or $5\frac{1}{2}$

7. Jim bought a toy soldier for $25. He later sold it for $20. How much money did he lose?

8. Complete the shading to show 1.56.

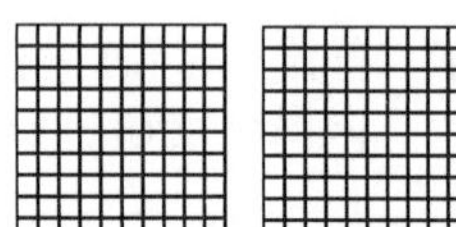

9. Select the best estimate:
A loaf of bread costs $1, $5 or $10.

10. How many eggs are in $3\frac{1}{2}$ dozen?

## Measurement and Geometry

11. February

| S | | 6 | 13 | 20 | 27 |
|---|---|---|---|---|---|
| M | | 7 | 14 | 21 | 28 |
| T | 1 | 8 | 15 | 22 | |
| W | 2 | 9 | 16 | 23 | |
| T | 3 | 10 | 17 | 24 | |
| F | 4 | 11 | 18 | 25 | |
| S | 5 | 12 | 19 | 26 | |

(a) Does this calendar show a leap year?

(b) Write the days and dates of the first weekend.

12. A fish tank filled with water weighs 23 kg. What would a tank double this size weigh?

13. Complete this table.

| *Length* | *Width* | *Area* |
|---|---|---|
| 5 cm | 3 cm | $cm^2$ |
| 4 cm | 2 cm | $cm^2$ |
| 3 cm | 3 cm | $cm^2$ |

14. Find two containers in your fridge that hold about 300 mL each.
1.
2.

15. This illustration suggests a high temperature. Make up a symbol of your own.

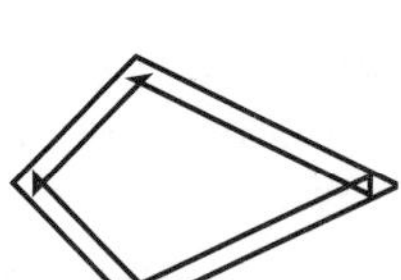

16. Where would you put extra strips of cardboard to make this model more rigid?

17. Name this solid shape.

18. Circle the largest angle.
(a) (b) (c)

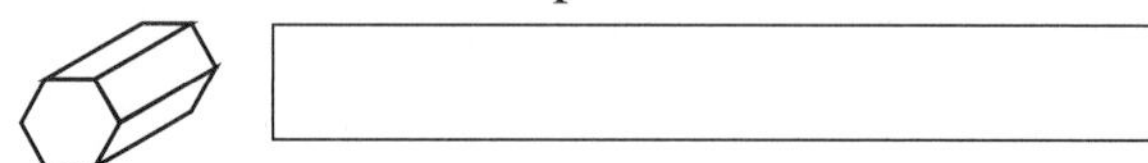

19. Continue this pattern by flipping the shape.

20. Use your ruler to draw a straight line from dot A to the smallest dot, then measure its length.

## Statistics and Probability

21. This represents a _ _ _ _ _ _ graph.

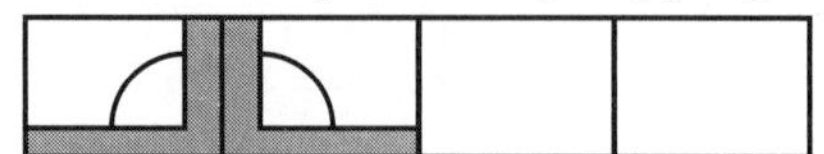

## I Wish I Was a Fish

"You two had better hurry up," called Mum. "It's nearly time to go."
"Coming, Mum!" I called back. I turned to my little brother, who was still tying his shoelaces.
"Come on, slowcoach. Do you want to be late? Mrs Cross will yell at you again."
Tommy finished his knot and ambled out to the kitchen. He grabbed a handful of biscuits.
"Put those back, young man," said Mum. "You won't be able to swim fast if you fill yourself with biscuits."
Tommy dropped the biscuits back on the plate. When Mum looked away, he slipped one into his pocket. She pretended not to see.
"Where's your towel?" asked Mum.
Tommy looked around and shrugged. "I don't know."
"I've got it," I shouted as I went out of the door. "Come on, Tommy."
"Wait a minute," said Mum. "What about your bathers?"
Tommy rolled back the top of his shorts to show that he had bathers on.
"Go on then, get going," said Mum. "Dad and I will see you there. Good luck! Swim as fast as you can!"
We walked quickly. Tommy kept up with me for a while, then started to lag behind.
"Hurry up, we're late now!" I said. I kept walking.

From *I Wish I Was a Fish* by John Fitzgerald

## Reading and Comprehension

1. A word with a similar meaning to *bathers* is
   (a) bathroom. (b) underpants.
   (c) togs. (d) shorts.

2. Which word in the extract tells you that Tommy was not in a hurry to get going?
   (a) slipped (b) ambled
   (c) shrugged (d) coming

3. What was the first question Mum asked the little brother?
   (a) Do you want to be late?
   (b) Where's your towel?
   (c) What about your bathers?
   (d) Hurry up! We're late now!

4. What is the contraction *won't* short for?

   ______________________________

5. Number these sentences in order (1–4).
   (a) He grabbed a handful of biscuits.
   (b) Mum wished us good luck.
   (c) Mum pretended not to see.
   (d) It was nearly time to go.

## Spelling and Vocabulary

Rewrite the misspelt words.

6. She woan't answer you until she is ready.

   ______________________________

7. My big sister mowed the lorn this morning.

   ______________________________

Circle the word that has the nearest meaning to the underlined word.

8. The toddler's disobedience was pushing her mother to the <u>edge</u> of her patience.
   (a) ever (b) everywhere (c) brink (d) rim

9. The dog was rather <u>cruel</u> to the little kitten.
   (a) nasty (b) catty
   (c) kind (d) bad

Circle the correct word in brackets.

10. The shopkeeper (neatly, neat) stacked the grocery items into the crate.

11. The (woman, women) offered me a glass of milk and I thanked her.

12. Does (anyone, everyone) know the tune which is playing on the radio?

## Grammar and Punctuation

13. Underline the **pronouns** in these sentences.

    Tony smiled as he raced inside to help his mother with the picnic hamper. Dad found his tartan rug and I grabbed my hat.

14. Punctuate and capitalise this sentence.

    isnt it a brilliant spring morning

    ______________________________

## Number and Algebra

1.

| + | 8 | 3 | 7 | 17 | 11 | 113 |
|---|---|---|---|---|---|---|
| 3 | | | | | | |

2.

| − | 13 | 9 | 15 | 18 | 20 | 120 |
|---|---|---|---|---|---|---|
| 3 | | | | | | |

3.

| ÷ | 30 | 12 | 15 | 9 | 21 | 99 |
|---|---|---|---|---|---|---|
| 3 | | | | | | |

4. Write the value of the underlined digit in 78<u>5</u>2.

5. Complete: 50, 100, 150, ___, ___, ___, ___

6. Draw a half of a ball here.

7. Take away $10 from this money. How much is left?

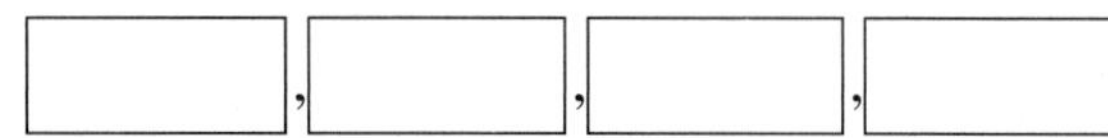


8. Cross out the smallest decimal fraction.
1.13, 1.03, 1.30

9. Select the best estimate.
Hair growth in a month : cm, m, km.

10. Write down three multiplications for getting 20.

1. ___ 2. ___
3. ___

## Measurement and Geometry

11. 1 year = ___ months

1 fortnight = ___ weeks

1 year = ___ weeks = ___ days

12. Circle the unit of length which would best suit measuring a bus: cm, m, km?

13. Complete this table.

| *Length* | *Width* | *Area* |
|---|---|---|
| 2 m | 2 m | $m^2$ |
| 4 m | 5 m | $m^2$ |
| 3 m | 6 m | $m^2$ |

14. A can of softdrink holds about:
50 mL, 350 mL or 700 mL.

15. Show 50°C on this thermometer.

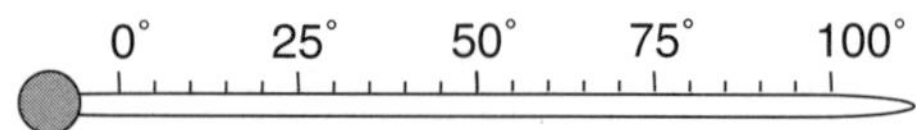


16. How many shapes make up this Tangram?

17. Draw a front view of a pram.

18. Draw three angles in order of size from largest to smallest.

19. A **flip** is like a ___________ in the mirror.

20. In the third box on the top floor, draw a pair of curtains.

## Statistics and Probability

21. This represents a ___________ graph.

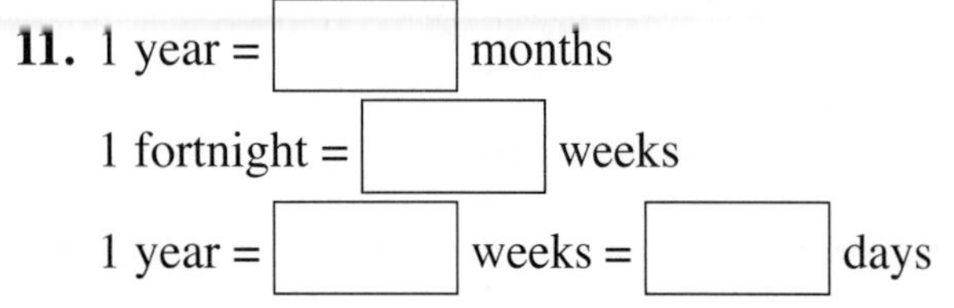

## Stevie Comes to Stay

Dear Joel,

Went to school today and it wasn't too bad at first. I could do all the reading and things but they have some funny Math. They call it 'sums' or 'arithmetic' or something. That's OK, but they measure things in millimetres, centimetres and metres, not inches, feet and yards. There are no miles either, just kilometres. I was getting the hang of that when they did history. It was about some explorer guys who found parts of Australia.

At lunchtime the kids were playing the greatest odd ballgame you've ever seen. It's called ~~criket~~ cricket, sort of like baseball but not the same.

I had to go as pitcher (they call him the bowler) and they said I did it wrong! There are lots of other rules and things that I can't work out yet. Who cares! I just got to tell you what the kids have on their sandwiches for lunch. It's black stuff that looks like tar and smells like it. One guy gave me a taste and it tastes like tar too! YUK! URK! The stuff is called ~~Vegamyt Vegamite~~ Vegemite and Aussie kids eat it ALL the time. Can't live without it. Doesn't seem to hurt them though. Some of them look pretty fit. I'm dying for some peanut butter and jelly.

My teacher, Mr Baker, wears short pants. You'd die laughing.

It's a bit lonely being the new kid at school. I sure wish you were here. There's a new girl in our class too. She comes from Thailand and can't speak English yet. Hope everything is going well over there. Did you get into the ice hockey team? I'll write next week. Stevie

From *Stevie Comes to Stay* by Gordon Winch

## Reading and Comprehension

1. Which word in Stevie's letter is similar to a *metre*?
   (a) feet (b) yard
   (c) inches (d) miles
2. What does Stevie loathe the taste of?
   (a) peanut paste (b) jelly
   (c) Vegemite (d) sandwiches
3. In which part of the world is Joel?
   (a) Australia (b) Austria
   (c) Northern Hemisphere (d) Thailand
4. Write the other word for *bowler* mentioned in the letter. ____________
5. Number these sentences in order (1–4).
   (a) Mr Baker wears funny, short pants.
   (b) Stevie has played a game of cricket.
   (c) Stevie will write again next week.
   (d) Some kids eat this black stuff.

## Spelling and Vocabulary

Rewrite the misspelt words.

6. Suzy had to wash the wollan jumper by hand.

   ____________

7. Every otha child had to go to the Music Room.

   ____________

Circle the word that has the nearest meaning to the underlined word.

8. Which sporting <u>ground</u> are you playing at next Saturday?
   (a) green (b) lawn (c) field (d) surface
9. He gave the Principal the correct <u>answer</u>.
   (a) response (b) replies (c) aid (d) assistance

Circle the correct word in brackets.

10. The girl in the red dress is Mary's (cousin, cousan).
11. Dr Gallows has (wrote, written) a prescription for you, dear.
12. If you like, I can (teach, learn) you how to make a glass picture.

## Grammar and Punctuation

13. Underline the **prepositions** in these sentences.

    She placed the plug in the hole and then filled the bath with warm water. On the vanity unit was the bar of soap. It slipped out of her fingers.

14. Punctuate and capitalise this sentence.

    dont forget to take your lunchbox shouted mum from the kitchen

    ____________

    ____________

## Number and Algebra

1.

| + | 8 | 10 | 3 | 6 | 12 | 70 |
|---|---|---|---|---|---|---|
| 7 | | | | | | |

2.

| – | 17 | 15 | 7 | 14 | 11 | 70 |
|---|---|---|---|---|---|---|
| 7 | | | | | | |

3.

| × | 10 | 3 | 5 | 8 | 2 | 70 |
|---|---|---|---|---|---|---|
| 7 | | | | | | |

4. Fill in the numeral expander for 6812.

☐ thousands ☐ hundreds ☐ ten ☐ ones

5. Write the next three numbers: 7303, 7304,

6. Colour part of this group to match $7\frac{1}{2}$.

7. Show $22.15 in the least amount of notes and coins.

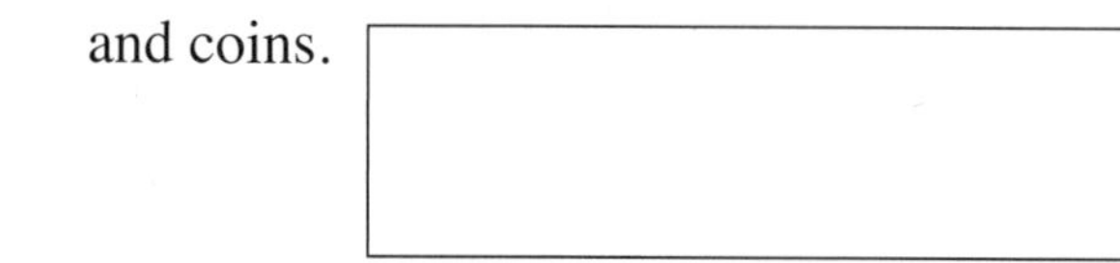

8. Write in decimal form:

(a) 1 and 15 hundredths

(b) 1 and 78 hundredths

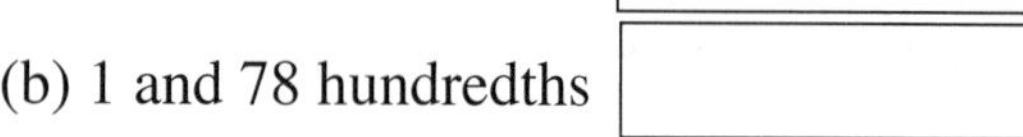

9. Select the best estimate.
Time it takes to eat lunch: 15 seconds, 15 minutes, 15 hours.

10. Mick spent half his money at the tuckshop. He then spent half of what was left at the grocery shop. If he has 20 cents left, how much did he start with?

## Measurement and Geometry

11. Circle the correct time measurement.
How long it takes to spend a day at the beach: seconds, minutes, hours, days

12. Find your height and write it in m and cm.

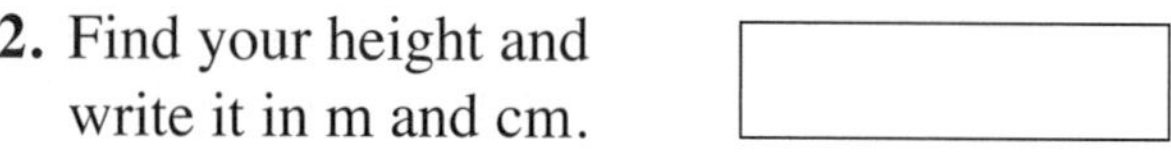

13. Circle the correct answer.
The area of a square with sides 5 cm is:
20 cm$^2$, 50 cm$^2$, 25 cm$^2$

14. True or False?
A bottle of nail polish contains 20 mL of liquid.

15. True or False?
It is not possible for the temperature to be 2°C first thing in the morning.

16. Tangrams were invented in _ _ _ _ _ about 4000 years ago.

17. Complete the copy of this model.

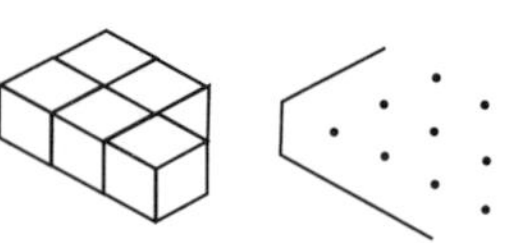

18. Draw a blunt angle.

19. Complete the basket of fruit.

20. (a) Who sits in 2, C?

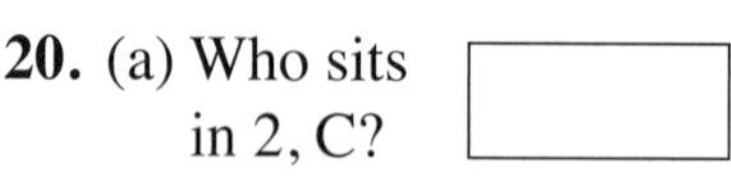

(b) Where does Jill sit?

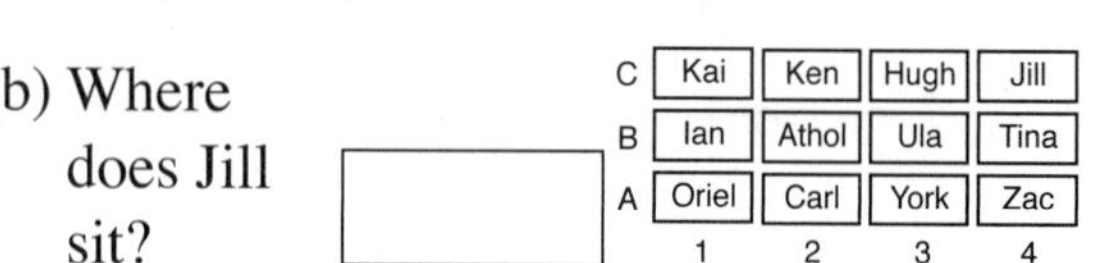

| | | | | |
|---|---|---|---|---|
| C | Kai | Ken | Hugh | Jill |
| B | Ian | Athol | Ula | Tina |
| A | Oriel | Carl | York | Zac |
| | 1 | 2 | 3 | 4 |

## Statistics and Probability

21. 卌 卌 卌 卌 卌 卌 卌 卌 |

(a) What tally is shown?

(b) Is it odd or even?

## A Modern-day Fable

The animals were standing around a barbecue boasting about their strength. Hare sprung up and said, "I have never been beaten in the backyard sprint!" He tossed another piece of carrot cake into his mouth. "I challenge anyone to race against me," he said as he threw off his thongs.

"Oh … I accept your challenge," whispered Tortoise. The animals stared at each other in disbelief. Lion threw another prawn on the barbie. "What a good one!" giggled Hare. "I could beat you hands down. Come on then Matey!" So the animals ambled to the backyard to witness this incredible event.

"On your marks, get set, go …" screamed Bear as he licked his honey lollipop. The animals were off. Tortoise plodded along, and along, and along. Hare was off as quick as lightning. Suddenly, Hare stopped. There was a mulberry tree in the middle of the yard. I'll just stop here and collect a few juicy ones, he thought. Tortoise won't catch me!

He sat near a bindy patch and commenced picking. Tortoise by now was about five centimetres away from the wooden fence. Just then, Hare looked up …

Moral: slow and steady wins the race.

## Reading and Comprehension

**1.** The word in the fable which means 'denial' is
(a) challenge. (b) plodded.
(c) commenced. (d) disbelief.

**2.** Which animal was the 'chef'?
(a) Hare (b) Tortoise
(c) Bear (d) Lion

**3.** What caught Hare's eye and distracted him from the race?
(a) a piece of carrot cake
(b) Bear's lollipop
(c) the mulberry tree
(d) the wooden fence

**4.** What does *commenced* mean?

______________________________

**5.** Number these sentences in order (1–4).
(a) Slow and steady wins the race.
(b) Tortoise accepted the challenge.
(c) Hare set up a challenge.
(d) The animals were enjoying a barbecue lunch.

## Spelling and Vocabulary

Rewrite the misspelt words.

**6.** The pharmacist handed me a bottle of coff medicine. ______________

**7.** The Swan Riva flows through the City of Perth. ______________

Circle the word from the list that has the nearest meaning to the underlined word.

**8.** Our netball team will play <u>against</u> your team on Sunday.
(a) about (b) around
(c) with (d) opposite

**9.** Hand me the longest golf <u>club</u> in the bag.
(a) racquet (b) stick (c) caddy (d) kit

Circle the correct word in brackets.

**10.** (May, Can) I borrow three cups of brown sugar, please?

**11.** The (new, knew) clock ticked (loud, loudly) on the brick wall.

**12.** With one puff I (blew, blow) out the (candle, candles) on my birthday cake.

## Grammar and Punctuation

**13.** Underline the **verbs** in these sentences.

Write the word in capital letters. Underline the vowels you see. Cross out the first letter using red biro. Erase the last letter. Check it!

**14.** Punctuate and capitalise this sentence.

i rang ian molloney to check on tonys progress

______________________________

______________________________

## Number and Algebra

1. Follow this addition path.

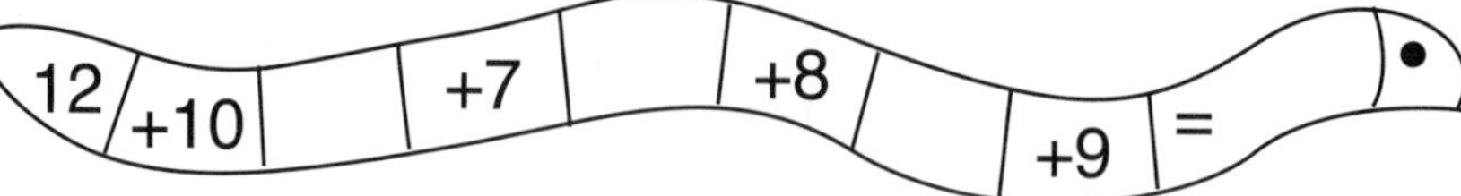


2. Follow this subtraction path.

3. Follow this division path.

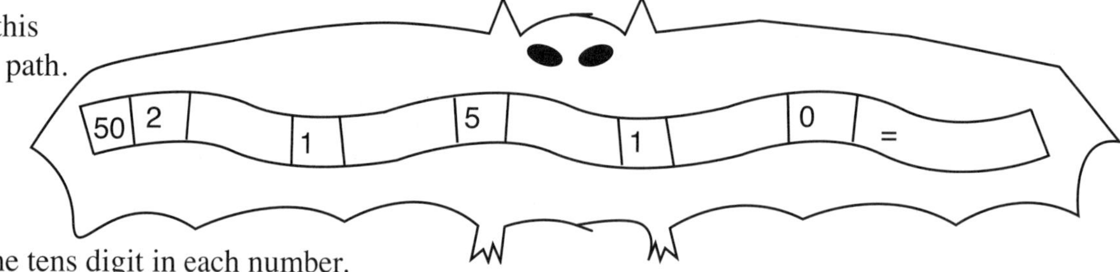


4. Circle the tens digit in each number.
   (a) 3962 (b) 4 075.6 (c) 9 001.99 (d) 7 555.5 (e) 18

5. Complete the sequences.
   (a) 1.75 m, 1.76 m, 1.77 m, ☐, ☐, ☐
   (b) $3.15, $3.10, $3.05, ☐, ☐, ☐

6. Which is bigger:
   (a) 2 and a half or 6 and a half? ☐ (b) 5 and a half or 3 and a half? ☐
   (c) 7 and a half or 1 and a half? ☐ (d) 6 and a half or 7 and a half? ☐

7. Answer the following money sums.

| (a) | (b) | (c) |
|---|---|---|
| $0.40 | $0.70 | $1.10 |
| $0.15 | $0.05 | $0.30 |
| + $0.30 | + $0.05 | + $0.40 |
| ☐ | ☐ | ☐ |

8. Find the decimal fraction of the shaded part.
   (a) ☐

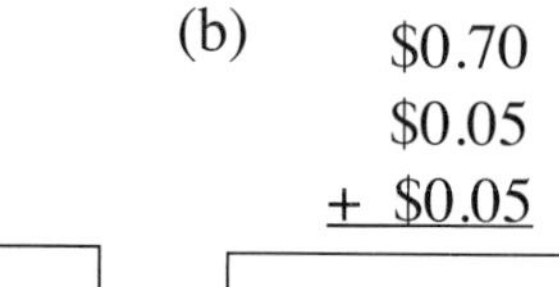

(b) ☐

9. Estimate the number in each set. Check by counting.

(a)

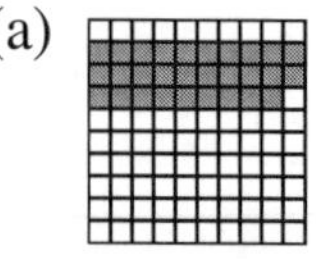

☐

(b)

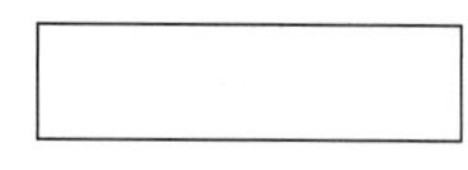

☐

(c)

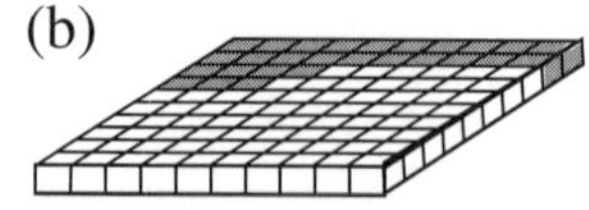

☐

(d)

☐

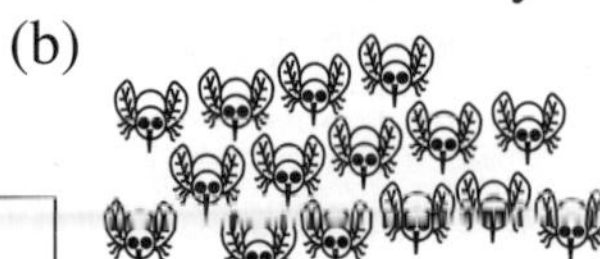

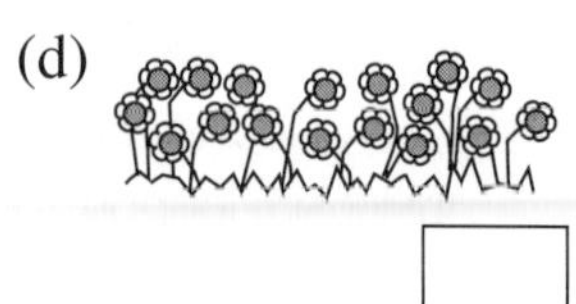

10. Each week a school tuckshop uses five 750 mL bottles of tomato sauce. How many litres of sauce would be used in 5 weeks? ☐

## Measurement and Geometry

**11.** Write a digital label for each time. (a)  (b)

**12.** A square carpet has a perimeter of 16 m. Find:

(a) the length of the side in metres (b) the distance halfway around the square

**13.** What is the area of this shape in square metres?

10 m

5 m

**14.** What is the volume of this model?

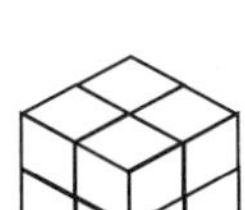

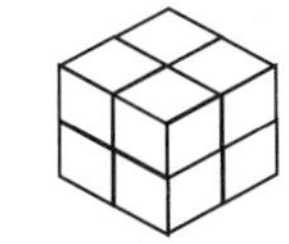

=1m³

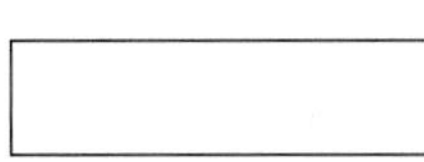

**15.** Put in the missing readings on the thermometer.

___° 20° ___° 60° ___° 100°

**16.** Join the dots, then name the plane shape.

**17.** Complete the table.

| *Name of Solid* | *Faces* | *Vertices* | *Edges* |
|---|---|---|---|
| Square Prism | | | |
| Cube | | | |
| Square Pyramid | | | |

**18.** How many degrees are there in a straight angle? 

**19.** Which picture shows: (a) a slide?
(b) a turn?
(c) a flip?

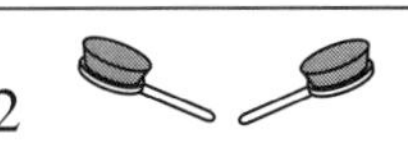


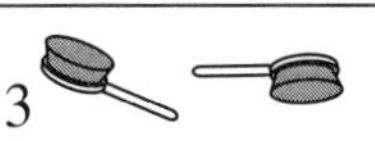


**20.**

(a) Which food item is on the top shelf? 

(b) Which item is third on the middle shelf?

(c) Name the only liquid item on the shelving.

## Statistics and Probability

**21.**

FRI
THU
WED
TUE
MON
0 1 2 3 4 5 6 7 8 9 10

This graph shows John's score in a tables test, held each day during the week.

(a) On which day did he get 10 out of 10?

(b) How many tables did he get wrong on Monday?

## Bird Facts

- A bird is any animal with feathers. Feathers are unique to birds. All adult birds have feathers. Pelicans and woodpeckers are born naked.
- Ostriches are the biggest birds. They grow up to 3 metres tall. They can't fly though.
- Most birds have relatively large eyes. They can perceive colours like human beings.
- Birds build a nest in which a female lays her eggs and then sits on them till they hatch.
- Some species of birds can be detrimental to humans, especially those that damage fruit and grain crops. Some have even caused aeroplane crashes.
- The smallest bird is the hummingbird. It weighs only about 2 grams.
- Extinction is a natural process of evolution. Since historical records have been kept, about 60 birds have become extinct.
- Birds have no teeth, so they swallow their food whole. Owls cannot digest the fur and bones of their prey.
- Swifts are the fastest birds and can move quicker than any other animal. They can fly up to 160 km/h!
- Birds inhabit every continent and almost every island in the world. They can adapt very easily to any environment.
- Sense of smell is only developed in some birds. Vultures can locate dead animals easily.

## Reading and Comprehension

1. Which word in the fact file means 'no longer existing'?
   (a) process
   (b) extinct
   (c) perceive
   (d) detrimental

2. Birds generally
   (a) have a keen sense of smell.
   (b) build nests.
   (c) are detrimental to human life.
   (d) grow up to 3 m tall.

3. The fastest bird around is the
   (a) vulture.
   (b) hummingbird.
   (c) owl.
   (d) swift.

4. About how many birds have become extinct since historical records have been kept?

   ______________________________

5. Number these words in alphabetical order (1–6).
   (a) pelican (b) owl
   (c) swift (d) vulture
   (e) hummingbird (f) ostrich

## Spelling and Vocabulary

Rewrite these sentences, correcting the misspelt words.

6. Vulturs can lowkate dead prey very easily.

   ______________________________

   ______________________________

7. A female laes her eggss and then sits on them.

   ______________________________

   ______________________________

Which word has the same, or nearly the same, meaning as the underlined word?

8. I was not able to <u>digest</u> all the information the teacher was reading to me.
   (a) indigest
   (b) discuss
   (c) dismiss
   (d) take in

9. The female sits on the eggs till they <u>hatch</u>.
   (a) bonnet
   (b) emerge
   (c) baby
   (d) eagle

Circle the word in brackets that fits the sentence.

10. Only I (know, knows) where the birdseed is.

11. I noticed that you (were, was) late to pick up your bird from the pet shop this morning.

12. Please (close, break, glue) the cage door!

## Grammar and Punctuation

13. Write the plural form of these words.

    bird ______________

    crop ______________

    tooth ______________

    ostrich ______________

14. Rewrite this sentence, correcting any spelling, capitalisation and punctuation errors.

    when the baby swiftt is redy to hach it beginz to moove inside the eeg the eegshell cracs the peices of shel fall of

    ______________________________

    ______________________________

    ______________________________

    ______________________________

Reprinted 1998, 1999, 2000, 2001, 2002, 2003, 2004, 2006, 2007, 2008 (twice), 2009, 2010, 2011 (twice)

**Updated in 2012 for the Australian Curriculum**

Reprinted 2014, 2015, 2016, 2018, 2019, 2020, 2021 (twice), 2023

ISBN 978 1 86441 275 8

Pascal Press
PO Box 250
Glebe NSW 2037
(02) 8585 4050
www.pascalpress.com.au

Publisher: Vivienne Joannou
Project editor: Mark Dixon
Australian Curriculum updates edited by Rosemary Peers and answers checked by Peter Little
Typeset by Precision Typesetting (Barbara Nilsson) and lj Design (Julianne Billington)
Cover by DiZign Pty Ltd
Printed by Vivar Printing/Green Giant Press



**Acknowledgements**
The following sources for material are kindly acknowledged:
*Great Dinosaurs* by Ross Latham and Peter Sloan
*Ho, Ho, Ho!* by Jan Weeks
*Pandas* by Christine Deacon
*Numbat, Run!* by Jill Morris and Lynne Tracey
*Jack Finds the Outback* by Judith Womersley
*Where's My Ticket*? by B Reinholdt and H Anderson
*Big April Fools*! by Edel Wignell
*My Diary* by Jenny Jarman-Walker
*A Night at Benny's* by Dianne Bates
*Adam's Boat* by Mary Small
*Show Off* by Hazel Edwards
*Going Fishing with My Dad* by Jan Weeks
*From the Land of Ikaros* by Petro Alexiou
*I Wish I Was a Fish* by John Fitzgerald
*Stevie Comes to Stay* by Gordon Winch.